THE

OF THE

DOUBLE PORTION ANOINTING

NANCY DUFRESNE

DUFRESNE MINISTRIES
PUBLICATIONS

The Price of the Double Portion Anointing
ISBN: 978-0-940763-47-0
Copyright © 2019 by Dufresne Ministries

Published by:
Dufresne Ministries Publications
P.O. Box 1010
Murrieta, CA 92564
www.dufresneministries.org

1-2500

Unless otherwise indicated, all Scriptural quotations are from the *King James Version* of the Bible.

Scripture quotations marked *Amplified* are taken from the *Amplified Bible,* Copyright © 1954, 1958, 1962, 1964, 1965, 1987 by The Lockman Foundation. Used by permission.

Printed in the United States of America. All rights reserved under International Copyright Law. Contents and/or cover may not be reproduced in whole or in part in any form without the express consent of the publisher.

Cover design: Nancy Dufresne & Grant Dufresne

WORLD HARVEST
BIBLE TRAINING CENTER

M U R R I E T A · C A L I F O R N I A

TRAINING BELIEVERS TO MOVE WITH THE WORD & THE SPIRIT

FOR MORE INFO OR TO SUBMIT AN APPLICATION ONLINE, GO TO

DUFRESNEMINISTRIES.ORG/whatiswhbtc

OR CONTACT OUR OFFICE AT (951) 696-9258, EXT. 202

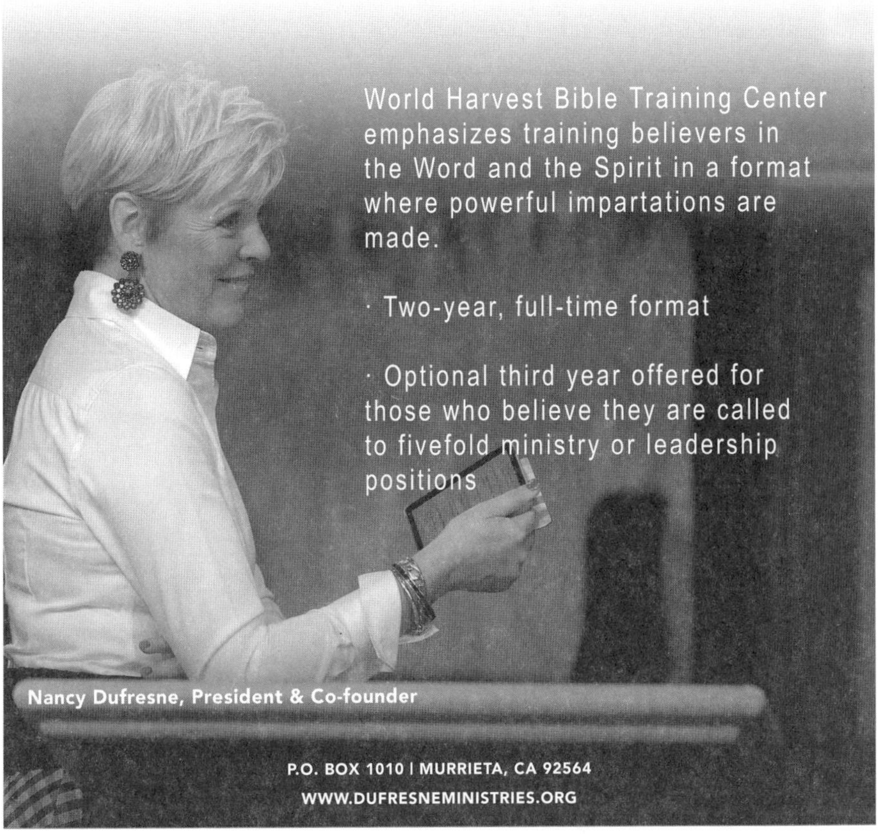

Books by Nancy Dufresne

A Sound, Disciplined Mind

Daily Healing Bread From God's Table

His Presence Shall Be My Dwelling Place

Victory in the Name

There Came a Sound From Heaven: The Life Story of Dr. Ed Dufresne

The Healer Divine

Visitations From God

Responding to the Holy Spirit

God: The Revealer of Secrets

A Supernatural Prayer Life

Causes

I Have a Supply

Fit for the Master's Use: A Handbook for Raising Godly Children

Knowing Your Measure of Faith

The Greatness of God's Power

Peace: Living Free From Worry

Following the Holy Spirit

An Apostle of the Anointing: A Biography of Dr. Ed Dufresne

Victory Over Grief & Sorrow

Answer It!

Contents

Dedication

It was my joyous privilege to run almost 30 years of my race alongside the man who was my companion, my Bible school, my mentor, and my husband, Dr. Ed Dufresne.

I and so many of those who called him "Dad" continue to run our race, endeavoring to show ourselves good students of his training, his example, and his life of faith.

To him and to those who imparted into both of us, I lovingly dedicate this book.

Introduction

Years ago, God said to me, "There are revelations that belong to this era, but you must labor in prayer to receive them." It's not about us trying to get God to *give* the revelations, but it's about us being in the position to *receive* the revelations He longs to give. As we take time in prayer, we position ourselves to receive into our spirits the revelations needed to advance in this era.

In different times and eras, there are certain truths that God will emphasize. For example, during the Azusa Street Revival of the early 1900s, there was an emphasis on being filled with the Holy Spirit with the evidence of speaking in other tongues. During the Healing Revival from 1947-1958, healing was the emphasis.

The revelations that belong to this era will give further light and clarity of God's Word that will enable us to move and operate accurately and skillfully in what God is emphasizing in this era.

In April of 2018, Jesus came into my hotel room in St. Petersburg, Russia, and talked to me for an hour about The Price of the "Double Portion" Anointing. I believe this is a revelation that belongs to this era, for it instructs us and gives clarity on how we are to walk successfully in this era.

Although this experience happened to me, it is not only for me – it is for the Body of Christ. It is up to us to receive it for our own lives.

In referring to the anointing, we must recognize that there is an anointing **within** and there is an anointing that comes **upon**.

The anointing that abides within every believer came in at the new birth and is for our own lives. Every believer has an equal measure of the anointing within, and the measure of that anointing within does not increase. Yet the more we yield to it, the more we will receive and benefit from it.

The anointing that comes upon is for those who are called and separated unto the ministry. It empowers them to stand in their offices and fulfill their ministries; this anointing is for ministering to others. The measure of this anointing can be increased; it can be increased by faithfulness, consecration, and diligence in the Word of God and prayer.

The title of this book, *The Price of the Double Portion Anointing,* came to me that night Jesus spoke to me. I realize that the "Double Portion" Anointing can only come when a man with the anointing exits the earth, and it can only come upon someone who was faithful to that man and followed him closely, just as it came upon Elisha at the exit of Elijah.

Again, Jesus spoke these things that night to me, so they will apply to me in a specific way. I realize that not everyone in the ministry will walk under a double portion of the anointing. However, those who have an anointing upon them for ministry can walk in an increased degree of that anointing, can learn to become more skillful with the anointing that is upon them, and can learn how to further cooperate and yield to the anointing so it can flow to its full potential power.

Although the message in this book instructs those in the ministry, it also brings instruction to every believer in helping them to fulfill the will of God for their lives.

Chapter 1

"I'm Going To Speak to You..."

It was May 5, 2018, on a Saturday evening that I was sitting around a dinner table in St. Petersburg, Russia, with some close minister friends of mine. We had just finished the service that night and had gone back to our hotel to have a late dinner at the restaurant. As we were nearing the end of the meal, the power of God became tangible as we sat at our table – so much so that I physically shook myself. Everyone at the table sensed it. We talked for about another 20 minutes, then we each went back to our hotel rooms.

As a couple walked with me to my hotel room, I was reminded of something God had said to me about two weeks prior to this trip. "I'm going to speak to you in Russia. I'm going to give you clarity."

For a time, there were some things I had been struggling with, and I knew I needed further clarity, so when He said He would give me clarity while in Russia, I was grateful and expectant. Since arriving in St. Petersburg on the previous Wednesday, I had kept my spiritual antenna up to see when He would speak to me. It dawned on me as I entered my hotel room that now was that time.

Once in my room, the power of God got stronger. I got pen and paper; I was ready to write. It seemed that Jesus was standing next to me. Then I realized that the power had become so strong in the restaurant because He had walked up to the table and stood by me. Now in my room, He began talking to me for the next hour, giving me the clarity He spoke of weeks before.

I want to share what He said to me that night. *What He talked to me about was The Price of the "Double Portion" Anointing.*

The Last Days Revival

Before I continue with what He said to me that night, I want to first state some things I had been praying and believing for regarding the Last Days Revival.

There are several things that my husband, Dr. Ed Dufresne, as well as other men of God had said by the Spirit about the Last Days Revival.

Some of the things they stated were:

1. This revival would contain all previous revivals wrapped up in one.
2. In this revival, all of the fivefold offices (apostle, prophet, evangelist, pastor, and teacher) would operate at 100% of their full potential power.

3. In this revival, all nine gifts of the Spirit would operate at 100% of their full potential power.

For a minister to operate at 100% potential of their office and for the nine gifts of the Spirit to flow at 100% of their potential power in a service, it's not just up to the minister, but it is also up to the congregation. Both the minister and the congregation must yield to, respond to, and cooperate with God. We all have to be taught how to yield to and cooperate with God.

Since it is God's plan that these fivefold offices and nine gifts of the Spirit operate at 100% of their full potential power, I was praying about that. One day the Spirit said to me, "Not many understand God's plan for this era, not many see what God is wanting to do. There is a great longing of the Father for people to **see** and **understand** Him and His plan. This can only be seen and understood by the Spirit."

That lets us know that these offices and gifts can't operate at their full potential power unless we see and know some things accurately.

I believe the things written in this book will help us to better see and understand Him and His plan for this era; they will help us with what we must know and do to become skillful and cooperate with God so that the fivefold offices and the nine gifts of the Spirit can operate at their full potential power.

I don't presume to say that what Jesus said to me that night is *all* that's involved in walking in the "Double Portion" Anointing, but it is what He emphasized that night.

He didn't spotlight faith, walking in love, living free from fear and worry, or other foundational truths of the believer's life, but I expound on in this book what He spoke to me about that night.

Keys for This Era

One minister told of the time as a little boy that his family accidentally left him behind in the house, locking the door behind them. When he realized they had left him, he screamed and kicked the door for a long time until he was badly bruised; he struggled to open the door, but he couldn't. Finally he laid down and fell asleep. He later awoke to the sound of the key unlocking the door. All the door needed was a key. All the struggling against the door was futile without the key.

I believe God is showing and will continue to show us keys to this era so that we don't struggle, but we get into the fullness of His plan for this era.

Cooperating With God's Power

For a period of time, I had been praying and believing for the full measure of the fivefold offices and the nine gifts of the Spirit to come into operation. I realized after He spoke to me that night in Russia that that would include the flow of the "Double Portion" Anointing. That's what belongs to this era, but we must know the price that this degree of anointing calls for.

Jesus paid the price to make that power available, but there is a price *we* must pay to walk in what He made available. It won't just fall on us automatically.

One minister told us of a time he was riding with another minister in a car when a crippled man crossed the street. He asked the other minister, "Is it the will of God to heal that man?"

"Yes," he answered, "if someone will pay the price."

What did he mean by that? He knew that Jesus had already paid the price for the man's healing, but he meant that someone was going to have to pay the price to become skillful with the healing power of God so that they could become a channel that God could heal through.

God's power blesses humanity, but that power flows through channels. By learning about God's power and becoming skillful with it, we can be those channels He can flow through so that humanity can be blessed. Power doesn't flow automatically. We must learn to cooperate with that power.

Electricity has been present upon the earth since the beginning of Creation, but even though it has always been present, it wasn't able to bring blessing to humanity until men begin to learn how to cooperate and conduct that power.

Power calls for skill. The greater the power, the greater the degree of skill that is required. To operate at 100% potential power, we must walk in that degree of skill.

Ready for the Lord

Luke speaks of John the Baptist.

LUKE 1:17 *(Amplified)*
17 And he will [himself] go before Him in the spirit and power of Elijah, to turn back the hearts of the fathers to the children, and the disobedient and incredulous and unpersuadable to the wisdom of the upright [which is the knowledge and holy love of the will of God] – in order to make ready for the Lord a people [perfectly] prepared [in spirit, adjusted and disposed and placed in the right moral state].

This last phrase stands out to me, "*...in order to MAKE READY FOR THE LORD a people [perfectly] prepared [in spirit, adjusted and disposed and placed in the right moral state].*"

We want to be "ready for the Lord" to use us in this era. So according to this scripture, the following things must be in place for us to be ready to be used:

1. Perfectly prepared in our spirits
2. Adjusted – having made needed adjustments

3. Disposed – which is defined as to put in a particular or the proper order or arrangement; adjust by arranging the parts, to put in a particular or suitable place; to make fit or ready; prepare
4. Be in a right moral state – moral excellence is a flow of a life of righteousness and is a companion of faith, and faith is required to walk out the plan of God for our lives and for this era, as well as to walk in the full measure of the anointing and grace upon our lives

What Jesus said to me in Russia will help ready us. It will help ready us for what's ahead in this era – the full potential of the fivefold offices and of the gifts of the Spirit – a "Double Portion" Anointing.

This revelation was given to me in two portions. The first portion He spoke to me on Saturday night (recorded in Chapter 2), but the next morning He gave me a second portion (recorded in Chapter 8), which is additional teaching He wanted me to give.

Opposition That Comes

What Jesus spoke to me that night was opposed. While He spoke, there came great opposition to my mind. Actually, the opposition started while we were in the restaurant, when Jesus came to the table.

There came negative thoughts bombarding my mind – one accusation after another coming as fast as machine gun bullets. The devil was trying to draw me and get me entrenched in the mental arena so I would miss what Jesus was saying to my spirit. For as Jesus spoke to me, I didn't see Him, I didn't hear Him with my outward ears, but I heard Him in my spirit. The enemy was trying to create much noise and distraction with bombarding thoughts in an effort to draw me away from my spirit into the mental arena. That's one of the primary strategies he uses against us.

God is a Spirit, so when He speaks to His children, He speaks to our spirits. What He says to our spirits will float up from our spirits and enlighten our minds; the words come up from within us. But when Satan speaks to us, he speaks to our minds. He speaks words from outside that come to and against our minds.

That night the enemy's words were coming against my mind, bombarding my mind from the outside. When God speaks, the devil is going to oppose that. He doesn't want you to recognize or receive what God is saying to you, or he wants to talk you out of that by getting you to reason in your mind against what God says to you.

Jesus said He has given His children the authority on the earth to deal with the devil. *"Behold, I give unto you power to tread on serpents and scorpions, and over all the power of the enemy: and nothing shall by any means hurt you"* (Luke 10:19). James 4:7 says, *"...Resist the devil [stand firm against him], and he will flee from you"* (Amplified). How do you resist him? You answer his threats and suggestions with what the Word of God says, then tell him to go!

A Strategy of the Enemy

Later I realized that God was preparing me for this visitation weeks before; He gave me a forewarning. To be forewarned is to be forearmed. Many times, God warns us ahead of time so we can be prepared to stand our ground against what the enemy plans to do.

God had said to me, "When the devil threatens you, accuses you, or tries to trouble your mind with a thought, he also produces a feeling in line with that thought to try to persuade you to believe what he's saying to you."

When God speaks to you, the anointing is then present to help you believe what He says to you. The devil imitates God, *so he also produces a feeling to try to persuade you to believe the wrong thing.*

What does it mean that the devil produces a feeling to try to persuade you to believe what he says? What he says to you can seem so real. For example, if he threatens you with something fearful, you will sense a feeling of great fear. If he condemns you with your past, you will sense a great feeling of condemnation, guilt, or shame. If he threatens you with thoughts of failure, you will sense a feeling of failure. He produces these feelings to try to persuade you to accept what he says to you.

No matter what the devil says to you and what you feel, answer him with the Word! Then tell him to go in Jesus' Name! Refuse to believe and accept the enemy's words or the feelings his words produce!

Even if the devil brings up something that you once did, once you repent, the blood of Jesus cleanses that away, so you are no longer guilty of it. Answer the devil, letting him know that you are forgiven and that that thing of the past no longer describes or pertains to you; refuse to accept any negative thoughts.

The devil is not going to stand back and just let what God says to you go unchallenged. He's going to bring opposition to try to get you off what God says. When you understand that, you're not swayed or impressed by that opposition, but you take your stand against it, refusing to yield to it. You are unimpressed by the enemy's strategies. You answer him – resist him, and he flees!

That night Jesus spoke to me in my hotel room in Russia, with His presence there was a great sense of reverence and awe. But at the same time, an evil spirit had come to try to interfere – it was trying to trouble and distract my mind. He pressed upon my mind, for he was trying to get me to disagree with what Jesus was saying. He accused me, saying that I could never meet the conditions Jesus was giving and that I would fail, so I shouldn't agree with Jesus. With those words also came all the feelings as though I couldn't meet Jesus' instructions and that I would fail. The sense of failure

I felt was great. But I have had enough experiences with the opposition of the enemy to recognize his strategy. This is what God had forewarned me of weeks before.

At the end of Jesus speaking, I spoke my agreement to Him, regardless of the overwhelming feelings of failure that the enemy was trying to press upon me, and when I did, that evil spirit left, and the whole atmosphere changed.

Anytime something troubles you, makes you fearful or doubtful, accuses you, condemns you, puts you down, or points to your weaknesses, faults, failures, or shortcomings, it's the devil trying to hold you back. Resist him and refuse to believe the feelings accompanying those words.

Chapter 2

The Price of the "Double Portion" Anointing

Although I had the visitation, it wasn't only for my benefit, but it is for the Body of Christ, for Jesus told me to put it in a book.

Don't make the mistake of assuming that what God shows you is only for you. Now, God may not release you to tell certain things, but if you are released to tell them, you should.

Many years ago, my husband became ill one night. When he asked God where he had opened the door to the devil, God told him that it was because he was not telling the visions he'd had to the Body of Christ as he should because he thought they were only for him. They weren't just for him. They were for him to tell to the Body of Christ.

Visions and revelations that have been given to other men of God were not just for them, but they are also *for* us – the Body of Christ. We are to be good stewards of them. We are to hold to them, tell them, and teach them to others and to future generations; answers for our lives, our future, and the plan of God are contained in them.

I believe that what Jesus spoke to me that night holds many answers for us all so that we can be prepared, ready, and skillful in flowing with God and His plan for this revival of the last days.

The Visitation

The following is most of what Jesus said to me that night:

> *To walk accurately and in the fullness of this era and season, do not misspeak under the anointing. Bring great consecration to the tongue and speech – not speaking lightly, inappropriately, or with exaggeration. Only truth can be in your mouth, for God and His power only flow through truth. I only said what I heard My Father say. I only did what I saw My Father do. You have the help you need for this task with the tongue through the Holy Spirit. The Holy Spirit will help you. Choose to have a guard set over your mouth, to have your tongue tamed by the power, help, and reliance upon the Holy Spirit. No man on his own can tame the tongue. It requires the divine help of the Holy Spirit.*
>
> *Slowness to make changes I deal with you about is unacceptable. There is to be* ***prompt obedience*** *to My correction, direction, and instruction. That slowness of change is a bad habit of the flesh that can be broken through the power of the Spirit. Walking in the Spirit is a requirement and a must for that change to take place.*

When Elisha asked for a double portion of the anointing upon Elijah, Elijah told him he asked a hard thing. It was not hard for God, but it would call for a hardness of Elisha toward his mind and flesh. He could not be tolerant toward weakness of his mind and flesh if he was to carry a double portion of the anointing.

You have called out for that place in the anointing, which God appreciates, but you must be sober about the responsibilities that anointing calls for. It pleases God to bless you with that anointing, but then it calls for you to be pleased to bring yourself in line with the responsibilities of that anointing.

Smith Wigglesworth is an example of the consecration and responsibility toward that anointing. He lived and walked in the Spirit with ease, freedom, and liberty as he spent his days in feeding and meditation on the Word and in fellowship with God through his ongoing devoted prayer life. Be mindful and purposeful to give yourself to the lifestyle of intake of the Word and fellowship with Me through continued prayer.

My yoke is light and easy. This can be accomplished with lightness and ease as you give yourself to focusing on these two things – continually feeding and meditating on the Word, and continual prayer and fellowship with God. Doing these two things will help you keep the door closed to the mind and the flesh, through which Satan and his strategies gain entrance.

Meditate often and much on the lightness and the ease of My yoke, that you think right toward these things.

In My presence is fullness of joy. Carry out My plan in My presence, then you will hold yourself in the joy of this flow – where the mind and the body are always kept under the dominion of your spirit (through continual intake of the Word & prayer).

Be an example in this, for you have the help of the greater One to carry this out.

There is no burden to the responsibilities of the anointing – as you take up your cross to follow Me, it ***lifts*** *you into the lightness and ease of* ***My*** *flow. I never conducted My earthly life as being under a burden of the price I was to pay. Life for Me was a great joy and delight. I only experienced being a Man of sorrows and acquainted with grief for a few brief moments on the cross. But I carried sorrows and griefs so that you would never experience it for a moment. In bearing it, I freed you from it so that you would only live your life under that which is light and easy.*

You need this to accomplish the fullness of My will. Now, move in it, and you will be lifted above that which tries to trouble you. As you walk daily in this direction, you will see difficulties and challenges fall off you.

I encourage you to prayerfully read and consider how to apply these things to your own life.

As I regularly read again these instructions He gave me, I don't just read through them, but I turn them into a confession that I make over my life (inserting "I" before each statement). For example, I confess it this way: *"I walk accurately and in the fullness of this era and season, and I do not misspeak under the anointing. I bring great consecration to the tongue and speech – I do not speak lightly, inappropriately, or with exaggeration. Only truth is in my mouth, for God and His power only flow through truth...."* Then I go throughout my day mindful to apply and do the instructions given, for they are not only a confession to make, but instructions to be carried out.

After speaking this to me, Jesus then gave me two words of knowledge regarding other people. I have noted that on other occasions when I have had experiences of Him visiting or dealing with me in a strong way, there would be words of knowledge or some other gift of the Spirit that would operate afterwards as a confirmation or a sign that God was speaking to me. This is in line with Mark 16:20, *"...confirming the word with signs following."*

In the following chapters, I will take each statement Jesus said to me that night and give further instruction along each line.

Chapter 3

Do Not Misspeak Under the Anointing

Jesus said to me that night, *"To walk accurately and in the fullness of this era and season, do not misspeak under the anointing. Bring great consecration to the tongue and speech – not speaking lightly, inappropriately, or with exaggeration. Only truth can be in your mouth, for God and His power only flow through truth. I only said what I heard My Father say. I only did what I saw My Father do."*

Let's look at the first sentence. *"To walk accurately and in the fullness of this era and season, do not misspeak under the anointing."*

To walk accurately would mean to walk as He would have us walk. That would include us being skillful. To be skillful in the era and season of the last days, we must not misspeak under the anointing – we must become skillful in our speech. I'm not referring to speaking grammatically correct, but I'm referring to speaking in line with the Word and the will of

God. We are to please the Lord in our speech; we are to say what He tells us to say, and we are to speak rightly at all times, especially when under the anointing.

To misspeak under the anointing will keep us from accuracy and from flowing in the fullness of what the era holds.

From my own personal experience, let me give you an example of what Jesus meant by "misspeaking under the anointing."

Years ago, I was asked to speak at an event where about 4,000 people would be in attendance, including city and state officials.

For weeks, a flu epidemic had been spreading through the region. Three days before the event, the devil said to me, "You're going to get the flu." I answered him, "No, I won't get the flu." He threatened me with a specific threat, and I answered him with a specific reply.

Two days later, I was conducting our midweek church service. Toward the end of the service, I started making a negative statement about a particular denomination, and when I started the statement, I sensed in my spirit the Holy Spirit strongly check me, trying to stop me from making the statement. But because I was midway through the sentence, I just went ahead and finished the statement anyway. I ended the service shortly after, then walked out of the sanctuary. From the time I left the sanctuary and walked into our hospitality room, full-blown flu symptoms were on me. I immediately realized that I had opened the door to the devil to put that on me.

When I disobeyed the Spirit and stepped out of love through making that statement, I had gotten onto the devil's territory, so then he had the right to attack me. Any step outside of love is a step into sin, which is the devil's territory, and when we get on the devil's territory, he has a right to attack us.

I drove home and sat down at my kitchen table. With every flu symptom on me, I prayed, "Father, Your Spirit rose up within me and checked me on what I was about to say. But because I was already midway through the sentence, rather than just stopping, I finished the statement and said what the Spirit was trying to stop me from saying. I disobeyed Your Spirit, so I can't plead ignorance or justice because I'm guilty. I recognize that Your Spirit tried to stop me, but I overrode Him. Since I can't plead justice, I plead mercy! I have that event in the morning that I must conduct. I can't miss it. I plead mercy!"

Then God answered me, "Alright, I'll give you mercy, but next Sunday morning you get up before your congregation and repent for what you said. And if you don't, every flu symptom will come back on you after the service."

"You have a deal!" I quickly agreed. As soon as I said that, every symptom immediately left me and I felt perfectly fine. I was so grateful.

The next morning, I did the event, and scores of people, even many public officials, were born again. The devil wanted to stop me from doing the event, so he was looking for an opportunity to attack me, and by making a statement that was outside of love, I had given him the opportunity. But thank God for His mercy!

The next Sunday, I kept my end of the deal with God. I was glad to get up and repent to the congregation for what I had said.

The Rewards of Repentance

When we miss it and sin, it's not weakness to acknowledge that and repent. God rewards repentance.

The prodigal son repented to his father, and when he did, the father blessed him by putting his robe and ring on him and by throwing a feast to celebrate his return. The son was rewarded for his repentance.

When we were born again, we repented for the life of sin we were living and God rewarded us by making us new creatures in Christ and bringing us into His family, blessing us with all the rights and privileges of sonship. Repentance is rewarded.

Repentance doesn't show someone to be weak, it shows them to be strong. When we repent, God can work on our behalf, but if we fail to repent, He can't. Repentance opens the door for Him to work, but failure to repent closes the door to Him. Holding to pride will keep us from repenting when we are wrong, but when we humble ourselves and repent, we are rewarded.

Do ministers say wrong things in the pulpit? Sure, because we're human and we miss it. Actually, ministers have more opportunity to miss it because we have more opportunity to be up in front of people.

Now, don't get into fear over this either and think that every time you say something that isn't quite right that you have to publicly repent for it. No, if you repent publicly over every little thing you say wrong, the congregation will lose confidence in you, but there are those times when your spirit convicts you or when God deals with you about making something right, then follow Him in that. Otherwise, just repent privately to God and look to Him to help you not repeat that mistake again.

I give you this example about where I sinned and missed God to illustrate to you what Jesus meant about not misspeaking under the anointing.

Sober About God's Power

The anointing is the greatest power in existence, and we can't handle it or operate in it carelessly or mindlessly. We must be sober about the greatness of God's power.

Years ago, God said something to me along these lines. "The greater the anointing, the smaller the margin for error."

As the anointing increases upon us, we become a greater target for the enemy, and he's looking for an opportunity to attack us. But as we walk in the light of the Word, we keep the door closed to him.

As one minister stated, "Others may, but you may not." Just because others may say or do something and seem to get by with it doesn't mean we can.

The anointing is the greatest power in existence, so we can't handle it lightly or irresponsibly. And when we consider that it's God's will for the nine gifts of the Spirit to operate at 100% of their potential power, that's a lot of power! We must be skillful in handling it.

Think of the great precautions and care those take who handle radioactive and atomic power. There is nothing careless in their handling of it because of the great dangers of it if mishandled – how much more the anointing!

Consecrated Speech

> Jesus said to me, *"To walk accurately and in the fullness of this era and season, do not misspeak under the anointing. Bring great consecration to the tongue and speech – not speaking lightly, inappropriately, or with exaggeration."*

The next phrase Jesus spoke to me tells us how to keep from misspeaking under the anointing. *"Bring great consecration to the tongue and speech – not speaking lightly, inappropriately, or with exaggeration."*

A consecrated life calls for a consecrated tongue, and a consecrated tongue calls for a consecrated, disciplined thought life. We must guard our thought lives to guard our tongues.

We must do as instructed in 2 Corinthians 10:5, *"Casting down imaginations, and every high thing that exalteth itself against the knowledge of God, and bringing into captivity every thought to the obedience of Christ."* If a thought is not in line with the Word of God, we must cast it down and refuse to turn it over in our thought lives.

To be consecrated means to "be set apart." Our mouths, tongues, and speech are to be set apart – set apart from wrong ways of speaking, ways we will not enter into or participate in. The "Double Portion" Anointing calls for a consecrated tongue and speech.

A consecrated tongue is a disciplined tongue – one that's under great control. If we misspeak in daily life, we are more likely to misspeak when ministering under the anointing, so we must discipline our tongues in daily life.

Wrong speaking and wrong words are an open door to the devil, and he can gain entrance there. James 3:2 tells us, *"For we all often stumble and fall and offend in many things. And if anyone does not offend in speech [never says the wrong things], he is a fully developed character and a perfect man, able to control his whole body and to curb his entire nature"* (Amplified).

In 1 Timothy 6:20, Paul writes, *"O Timothy, guard and keep the deposit entrusted [to you]!* (Then Paul tells Timothy how to keep the deposit that is entrusted to him.) *Turn away from the irreverent babble and godless chatter, with the vain and empty and worldly phrases..."* (Amplified).

Having been around some of God's generals in the Body of Christ, it was easy to see that they were not men who spoke loosely or carelessly. These men of faith knew that their words were *spiritual currency* – their words purchased things – so they didn't speak mindlessly and spend their words loosely. Their words carried power and purpose.

They didn't try to sound spiritually deep – they were so naturally themselves. They were warm, friendly, engaging, and personal, and they spoke easily with others, yet their spirits were so large and full of God that there was weight to their words and conversations. Their words were measured; they didn't spend them lightly.

Charles Finney, a minister of the 1800s, had great revivals that had a tremendous impact on this nation. Father Nash, a man known for his prayer life, would arrive in the towns where Charles Finney was to conduct a revival and would spend days in prayer for the meetings. When Charles Finney was asked what Father Nash was like, he said, "He doesn't talk much, like any man who prays a lot." When a man understands his place with God, he is sober about the value and power of right words.

When Jesus said to me, *"Bring great consecration to the tongue...,"* He then told me how to do that, by *"...not speaking lightly, inappropriately, or with exaggeration."*

"...Not Speaking Lightly..."

Growing up, I was quick to use wit to get an upper hand and to try to get the last word in a situation. But decades ago, God dealt with me strongly that using wit to gain the advantage would not only negatively affect my marriage and other relationships, but would hinder my spiritual development.

When God dealt with me about it, I told Him that I didn't realize how wrong that was, and since I had been doing it for so long, it might take me a while to get that changed.

He answered me, "I'm not giving you a while to change it. The way to change it immediately is, if you wouldn't say it, think it, or do it to Jesus, then don't say it, think it, or do it to anyone else." He was right. When I thought of it like that, that bad habit was changed quickly.

Now, I believe in having fun and enjoying conversations with people, but there is a point where a line is crossed and it isn't pleasing to the Lord, thereby hindering spiritual growth and development.

We must discipline ourselves to not speak lightly or mindlessly. My mother used to tell us kids, "Quit rattling!" Just because there's silence doesn't mean it has to be filled.

"...Not speaking inappropriately..."

Inappropriate speaking would be words of fear, doubt, anger, jealousy, strife, offense, gossip, combativeness, speaking disrespectfully or dishonorably, being critical or judgmental, and all sins of the mouth. It would include off-color jokes or conversations, speaking inappropriately with or about the opposite sex, speaking about things that aren't our business, as well as giving our opinion about something over which we have no authority.

But inappropriate speaking would also include being irreverent toward spiritual things – joking about spiritual things in general and joking about spiritual things that take place in a service.

If parents speak against others in front of their children, wrong things will get in their children. If they speak against the church leadership and congregation members, their children will lose all regard and honor for the church and church leadership.

Some of the most dangerous speaking is that of speaking against spiritual leaders and fellow Christians. Anything that would cause harm or division in the Body of Christ or in a local church is dangerous and must be guarded against.

Years ago, one minister addressed the dangers of speaking against others. He gave this illustration. "If you took a bag of feathers up to the top of a mountain and then shook them out in the wind, the wind would carry them everywhere and you would never be able to get them all back. Even so, when you speak wrong words about others, those words are like feathers – they are carried everywhere. Even if you repent,

God will forgive you, but you can never gather back up the effects of those words."

When I started pastoring in 1991, God taught me how to help our congregation regarding gossip. If you tell information you have to someone who has the authority to help or address that situation, then you're protecting people. But if you tell it to someone without the authority to help or address the situation, then you're gossiping, even if you're telling it to a spouse or family member.

To keep from speaking inappropriately requires us to pay attention and be disciplined toward our thoughts and our words.

"...Not speaking with exaggeration..."

Smith Wigglesworth, a minister from England, stated, "Exaggeration is not truth, and God can only bless truth." Exaggeration can be a bad habit that must be dealt with. We must all discipline ourselves to tell something without embellishing it with exaggeration.

I've heard the phrase, "Evangelistically speaking...," regarding someone telling the numbers in attendance or the results in a church service, but that shouldn't be associated with a minister or a ministry. Give accurate numbers and accurate results in your ministry, for God can only bless truth.

Exaggeration about something never makes it true, but it can ruin the credibility of a person or a ministry.

Power Flows Through Truth

> Jesus said to me that night, *"Only truth can be in your mouth, for God and His power only flow through truth."*

Truth must be in our mouths in the pulpit, as well as in our personal lives. In 2 Timothy 4:2, Paul instructed Timothy, *"Preach the word...."* The Word is truth, and God and His power can only flow through truth, but the devil can enter where there's not truth.

We're not to preach opinion or conviction. As one minister stated, "Don't preach your convictions, but you had better have them!"

God may deal with us about something in our life, but that doesn't mean we make that conviction a doctrine to preach to others, for God may lead somebody else differently.

To have God's power flowing, we have to weed anything out of our preaching that isn't in line with the Word. The Holy Spirit works with the Word, and when the Word is preached, then His power can meet that Word.

Mark 16:20 reads, *"And they went forth, and preached every where, the Lord working with them, and confirming the WORD with signs following...."* Jesus only confirms the Word with signs following, not opinions or convictions.

The Amplified translation of Proverbs 8:8 reads, *"ALL the words of my mouth are righteous (upright and in right standing with God); there is NOTHING contrary to TRUTH or CROOKED in them."* We are to speak truth in the pulpit, as well as truth in everyday life. "ALL the words..." of our mouths are to be righteous.

When Jesus stood in front of the grave of Lazarus, He *"...lifted up His eyes and said, Father, I thank You that You have heard Me. Yes, I know You ALWAYS hear and listen to Me..."* (John 11:41 & 42, Amplified). God didn't just hear Jesus three days earlier when He said, "...This sickness is not unto death..." (John 11:4), but He heard Him *always*.

God doesn't just hear us when we're directing our words to Him, but He also hears us when we're directing our words to others – our spouse, our family, our co-workers, the clerk in the store, the other drivers on the freeway, etc.... In all places and in all conversations, truth must be in our mouths.

Any wrong talk about situations or other people is not truth. Giving opinions is not truth. Gossip is not truth. We must discipline ourselves to only speak in line with truth, for God can only flow through and bless truth.

Facts Vs. Truth

There is a difference between facts and truth. Facts deal with this natural realm and are subject to change. Truth deals with the Word of God and never changes.

Facts are that which may be printed in a paper or heard on a newscast, but can change daily or from moment to moment. Truth is that which never changes.

Circumstances around our lives are facts, for they can change, but the truth of the Word remains constant and unchanging.

It may be a fact that you feel pain or symptoms in your body, but the truth of God's Word is higher than facts, and truth trumps facts! The truth is that Jesus took our infirmities and bare our sicknesses (Matt. 8:17). When you speak the Word, you lay the truth of God's Word on the facts of those symptoms, and the truth changes the facts. Truth trumps facts!

It may be a fact that there is not enough money in your bank account to pay the bills that are due, but God says to the giver that He will supply all your need according to His riches in glory by Christ Jesus (Phil. 4:19). When you speak the Word, you lay the truth of God's Word on those finances, and the truth changes the facts.

Any fact that is contrary to the truth of the Word is to be overridden with the Word. We are authorized to override the facts and circumstances of our lives with the truth of the Word. As we put our attention on the Word and confess words of truth over our situation, the truth will change the facts.

Focusing on and talking about circumstances and facts is not truth. To walk in the "Double Portion" Anointing, our thoughts, attention, and words must be held on truth and not on facts. As Proverbs 8:8 instructs us, there is to be "...nothing contrary to truth or crooked..." in our words.

Divine Help With the Tongue

> Jesus said to me that night, *"I only said what I heard My Father say. I only did what I saw My Father do."*

Jesus didn't use the influence He had with the people to express Himself, His own thinking, and His own opinions; He only spoke and did what was authored by His Father. Jesus was disciplined in His thought life and in His speech.

> Jesus went on to say to me that night, *"You have the help you need for this task with the tongue through the Holy Spirit. The Holy Spirit will help you. Choose to have a guard set over your mouth, to have your tongue tamed by the power, help, and reliance upon the Holy Spirit. No man on his own can tame the tongue. It requires the divine help of the Holy Spirit."*

We cannot control and dominate our tongue with human willpower; we have divine help for that – the help of the Spirit of God. But as Jesus said to me that night, we must *choose* to have a guard set over our mouths. We can choose to yield to the Spirit or choose not to yield to Him when He is endeavoring to help us. We yield to Him by responding to Him and His leading.

Psalm 141:3 reads, *"Set a guard, O Lord, before my mouth; keep watch at the door of my lips"* (Amplified). The Word and the Holy Spirit are guards to help us keep watch over our mouths; they will direct us in our speaking. But we must give place to and listen to them, not ignoring them or overriding them when the Word and the Spirit check us.

James 3:8 reads, *"But the tongue can no man tame...."* No man can tame the tongue with a natural force, but the Word of God can tame it when you get the Word in you and in your mouth.

Romans 8:13 tells us *"...ye **through the Spirit** do mortify the deeds of the body...."* The Amplified translation reads, *"...through the power of the [Holy] Spirit you are [habitually] putting to death (making extinct, deadening) the [evil] deeds prompted by the body...."*

Through the Spirit – praying in the Spirit – we have help in bringing the tongue under control. As we pray in the Spirit, our spirits are strengthened to rise up and dominate our flesh, thereby helping keep the tongue under control. What a divine help that is to us.

Chapter 4

Prompt Obedience

Jesus stated to me that night, *"Slowness to make changes I deal with you about is unacceptable. There is to be **prompt obedience** to My correction, direction, and instruction. That slowness of change is a bad habit of the flesh that can be broken through the power of the Spirit. Walking in the Spirit is a requirement and a must for that change to take place."*

First Corinthians 8:3 tells us, *"But if one loves God truly [with affectionate reverence, **prompt obedience**, and grateful recognition of His blessing], he is known by God [recognized as worthy of His intimacy and love, and he is owned by Him]"* (Amplified).

One way we demonstrate our love for God is through our prompt obedience.

Second Corinthians instructs us,

2 CORINTHIANS 9:7 *(Amplified)*
7 Let each one [give] as he has made up his own mind and purposed in his heart, not reluctantly

> **or sorrowfully or under compulsion, for God loves (He takes pleasure in, prizes above other things, and is unwilling to abandon or to do without) a cheerful (joyous, "PROMPT TO DO IT") giver [whose heart is in his giving].**

If God wants promptness of obedience in our giving, He would certainly want promptness of obedience in every arena of our life.

Proverbs reads,

> **PROVERBS 10:17 *(Amplified)***
> **17 He who HEEDS instruction and correction is [not only himself] in the way of life [but also] is a way of life for others. And he who NEGLECTS or REFUSES reproof [not only himself] goes astray [but also] causes to err and is a path toward ruin for others.**

To "heed" instruction and correction is to listen and obey; when we obey, we walk in the way that blesses our lives and the lives of others. But to "neglect" to do right is just as dangerous as "refusing" to do right. Sometimes, we don't intend to be neglectful, but the outcome of neglect still affects us and others negatively.

We are not to be neglectful or slow to obey, but be prompt to obey.

Chapter 5

Hardness Toward the Mind & Body

Jesus stated to me that night, *"When Elisha asked for a double portion of the anointing upon Elijah, Elijah told him he asked a hard thing. It was not hard for God, but it would call for a hardness of Elisha toward his mind and flesh."*

If we are to walk under a double portion of the anointing or under a full measure of the anointing available to us, we must do the right thing with our minds and our bodies so that our spiritual lives can develop as they ought. How we handle our minds and bodies will either accelerate or hinder our spiritual development – qualify or disqualify us.

We are a spirit, we have a soul (made up of the mind, the will, and the emotions), and we live in a body. When a man's spirit is right toward God, his spirit wants God's will, but the body will want to do wrong; the body will oppose the spirit.

The only variable left is the mind. If the mind sides with the body, the body will dominate over the spirit, but if the mind sides with the spirit, the spirit will dominate the body. Whichever one the mind sides with will dominate.

If the mind is renewed, it will side with the spirit, and the spirit will dominate the man. But if the mind is left unrenewed, it will side with the body, and the body will dominate the man.

When we were born again, God did something with our spirit – He gave us a new spirit. Ezekiel reads,

> **EZEKIEL 36:26 & 27**
> **26 A new heart also will I give you, and a new spirit will I put within you: and I will take away the stony heart out of your flesh, and I will give you an heart of flesh.**
> **27 And I will put my spirit within you, and cause you to walk in my statutes, and ye shall keep my judgments, and do them.**

God gave us a new spirit, but we still have the same mind and body we had before we were born again. We are the ones who must do something with our minds and our bodies.

Keeping Our Bodies Under

Romans 12:1 tells us what to do with them. *"I beseech you therefore, brethren, by the mercies of God, that ye* ***present your bodies*** *a living sacrifice, holy, acceptable unto God, which is your reasonable service."*

This passage instructs us to present our bodies to God. We are to rule over our bodies; they are not to rule over us. We are the master over our bodies, otherwise we couldn't present them to God.

We are to present our bodies to God; we are no longer to present our bodies to sin or to wrongdoing, but present them to God.

What does it mean to present our bodies to God? We are to yield our bodies to God by responding to what He tells us to do with them. If someone is presenting or yielding their body to sin, they are yielding their body to what is wrong. But we are to present our bodies to God by yielding to and responding to what God says is right and no longer present our bodies to sin by yielding and responding to wrongdoing with our bodies.

Romans 6:13 shows this clearly. *"Do not continue offering or yielding your bodily members [and faculties] to sin as instruments (tools) of wickedness. But offer and yield yourselves to God..."* (Amplified).

In 1 Corinthians 9:27, Paul tells us what he did regarding his body. *"But I keep under my body, and bring it into subjection: lest that by any means, when I have preached to others, I myself should be a castaway."*

The body of this apostle of God still wanted to do wrong; that's why he had to keep it under.

When Paul said, "But I keep under my body, and bring it into subjection...," the "I" he was referring to was his spirit man, and he called his body "it." So, he was saying that he kept his body under the dominion or control of his spirit. He didn't allow his body to take the lead in his life; he didn't allow his body to lead him into wrongdoing.

If anyone allows their body to lead them, it will lead them into ruin because the body wants to do wrong. That's why we have to keep the body under the control and dominion of our spirit.

The Amplified translation of this verse states this clearly.

1 CORINTHIANS 9:27 *(Amplified)*
27 But [like a boxer] I buffet my body [handle it roughly, DISCIPLINE IT by hardships] and SUBDUE IT, for fear that after proclaiming to others the Gospel and things pertaining to it, I myself should become unfit [not stand the test, be unapproved and rejected as a counterfeit].

Paul stated that if he didn't keep his body under control, he would be a "castaway" (KJV). The Amplified translation says he would *"...become unfit [not stand the test, be unapproved and rejected as a counterfeit]."* Another translation states that he kept his body under the dominion of his spirit so that he wouldn't be "...set aside as unusable."

This lets us know that if we allow our bodies to lead and dominate our lives, God will be unable to use us as He wants. But that doesn't have to be the case. We can be dominated and led by our spirits rather than by our bodies.

Jesus told His disciples, *"Watch and pray, that ye enter not into temptation: the spirit indeed is willing, but the flesh is weak"* (Matt. 26:41). As we spend time in God's presence, the spirit is fortified to keep the body under the dominion of the spirit.

The flesh won't want to do what's right. The flesh won't want to pray, but the spirit is to rule the body and lead it to do the right thing.

One pastor told of the time he had a young evangelist in to preach for him. Because he was young, he would spend the days out fishing and hanging out with the other young adults from the church. So in the afternoon, the pastor would go out and get him, telling him it was time to come in and pray and get ready for the service. Because this young evangelist was letting his body rule him, the older pastor was helping him put his flesh down.

Renewing of the Mind

To be dominated by our spirits, we not only have to do something with our bodies, but we must also do something with our minds.

Romans 12:1 tells us what to do with our bodies, but verse 2 goes on to tell us what we are to do with our minds. *"And be not conformed to this world: but be ye* ***transformed*** *by the* ***renewing of your mind****, that ye may prove what is that good, and acceptable, and perfect, will of God."*

To "renew the mind" means to take on God's thoughts – to think like God thinks. The Word of God is the thoughts of God. As we read the Word, we find out how God thinks. When we see something in the Word that is different than the way we were taught to think, we are to lay aside our way of thinking and take on His way of thinking, then we are to implement those thoughts into our everyday life – they are to govern and direct us in our everyday life.

It's not enough to know what He says and know how He thinks – we must do what He says. His Word must govern our daily lives. We must take His thoughts and make them our own so that we live them. The mind is not renewed until we are thinking God's thoughts and living our lives in line with them.

We must daily renew our minds with the Word of God because the mind doesn't stay renewed any more than the hair stays combed. Just as we put our hair in place every day, we must feed on God's Word daily to keep right thinking in place.

As we renew our minds with the Word of God, we think and act in line with God's Word. It also enables us to recognize wrong thoughts that the enemy suggests so that we keep the door closed to them.

Guarding Our Thought Lives

The mind is Satan's battleground. The devil gains entrance and defeats us through wrong thinking. That's why we must renew our mind with God's Word, so we will recognize wrong thoughts and not let them in.

Satan suggests wrong thoughts, and if he can get us thinking about them, turning them over and over in our thought lives, he can whip us. That's why he seeks to hold us in the mental arena – because if he can, he will whip us. But if we hold him in the spirit arena, the faith arena, we will whip him.

He will try to bombard our minds with wrong thoughts, and if we turn them over and over in our minds, they will get in. But we don't have to let them. We are to answer those wrong thoughts with the Word, then turn our attention and focus away from what he says by turning our attention to God by praising and worshipping Him, for that holds us out of the mental arena and in the spirit arena.

Just because the devil bombards our mind doesn't mean that he's gotten in. We may hear someone continually knocking on our front door, but that doesn't mean they have gotten into our house. And just because we can hear them knocking doesn't mean we have to open the door to let them in. It's the same thing with the devil – just because he's bombarding our mind with wrong thoughts doesn't mean he's gotten in, and it doesn't mean we have to let him in.

We must stay out of the mental arena, the thinking arena, the reasoning arena. If the devil can get us thinking about things, trying to reason things out, he can whip us.

That's how he whipped Eve – he got her thinking about what he said to her. She started listening to him, and when she listened long enough, what he said started making sense to her. If we listen to wrong thoughts long enough, they will start making sense to us, and we will open the door to the devil.

But if we opened the door to the devil, we can close the door to the devil, by refusing to take and act on the thoughts he suggests.

We must guard and discipline what we allow our minds to think on.

Philippians tells us what to think on.

PHILIPPIANS 4:8
8 Finally, brethren, whatsoever things are true, whatsoever things are honest, whatsoever things are just, whatsoever things are pure, whatsoever things are lovely, whatsoever things are of good report; if there be any virtue, and if there be any praise, think on these things.

We must practice thinking on these things, for practice is how we become skillful at guarding our thought lives.

We are not to allow our minds to rule us; our spirits are to rule us.

The Help of the Holy Spirit

We have divine help in keeping our bodies and flesh under the dominion of our spirits. Romans 8:13 tells us *"...ye **through the Spirit** do mortify the deeds of the body...."*

The Amplified translation reads, *"...**through the power of the [Holy] Spirit** you are [habitually] putting to death (making extinct, deadening) the [evil] deeds prompted by the body...."*

Praying in the Spirit helps us keep our bodies under control. As we pray in the Spirit, our spirits are strengthened to rise up and dominate our flesh, thereby helping keep the body under control.

Before my husband was born again, he worked as a carpenter. For a year and a half, a co-worker invited him to church every week. Each week, my husband would turn him down using some very colorful language. Finally, my husband said to him, "If I go to church with you once, will you leave me alone?"

"Yes," he agreed, "I'll leave you alone."

So Ed went to church with him the following Sunday and was born again. He immediately began serving in the local church, then went on into full-time ministry, serving God for 48 years.

But after being born again, Ed asked his co-worker, "Is something wrong with you physically? I noticed that you go to the restroom a lot when you're working on the job."

"No, there's nothing wrong with me," he answered. "But every time I would invite you to church and you would cuss me out, I would go into the restroom and pray in other tongues just so I could keep from hitting you."

His co-worker understood that by praying in other tongues, it strengthened his spirit so that he could keep his flesh under control. That's one of the great benefits of speaking in other tongues – it will help us keep our flesh from dominating us.

Instead of responding wrongly, take time to speak in other tongues, and you'll be accessing the divine help that is always available to the Spirit-filled believer.

By living and walking in the Spirit, we can keep the body in its rightful place – under the dominion of our spirit.

Romans 8:4 instructs us, *"...live and move not in the ways of the flesh but in the ways of the Spirit [our lives governed not by the standards and according to the dictates of the flesh, but controlled by the Holy Spirit]"* (Amplified).

First Corinthians 14:4 tells us, *"He that speaketh in an unknown tongue edifieth* (builds up) *himself...."* As we speak in other tongues, our spirits are built up and strengthened. When our spirits are built up, they will be strengthened to keep our bodies under control.

Developing & Following Our Spirits

We must develop our spirits by feeding on the Word of God (which is faith food for our spirits), by acting on that Word in daily life, and by fellowshipping with God in prayer.

God leads us through our spirits, not through our minds, feelings, emotions, or outward circumstances. And the more sensitive we are to our spirits, the more we will recognize what His Spirit is saying to our spirits.

We make our spirits sensitive to the Holy Spirit as we take time to speak in other tongues. To recognize how He is leading us and to follow the Spirit *accurately,* we must take time to speak in other tongues. It's a spiritual habit we can develop by taking every opportunity to speak in tongues as we go about life's daily duties – while getting dressed, running errands, driving to work, etc.

As we speak in other tongues, what our spirit knows will float up from within and enlighten our minds, but if our minds are racing, cluttered, and busy, we will miss what our spirits are trying to communicate to us. So, we must become skillful at quieting our minds and focusing on our spirits so that we can receive the full benefit of speaking in tongues.

To quiet your mind, put your mind in neutral, not thinking anything, or put your mind on Jesus, and focus on your spirit as you speak in other tongues. The more you practice this, the easier it will become and the quicker you will get in the Spirit. And it's when you deal with things from that place in the Spirit that you get results.

To live in the Spirit, we must practice turning our attention toward our spirits instead of toward our minds, and to do that, we have to learn to discipline and quiet our minds.

As we daily live full of the Word and the Spirit, we are able to walk out our lives in the Spirit, which is the life He authored for the New Testament believer.

Years ago, God said to me, "Start every day in the Spirit, then keep your heart turned toward Me all day long." This will help us to stay mindful of Him all throughout the day, and as we are mindful of Him, it can't help but affect the way we live.

Yes, it takes practice to become skillful at it, but as we take time to do it, we can accomplish living in the highest sense – in the Spirit.

Not Tolerant Toward Any Weaknesses

> Jesus said to me that night in Russia, *"He* (Elisha) *could not be tolerant toward weakness of his mind and flesh if he was to carry a double portion of the anointing."*

To walk in the "Double Portion" Anointing, we cannot be tolerant and permissive toward weakness of our minds and flesh. We must renew our minds with God's Word and keep our bodies under the control of our spirits. We cannot allow the mind and the body to dominate us; we must pay strict attention to what we allow in our thoughts, words, and actions.

We can live the best life as we feed, develop, and yield to our spirits. It is possible to live the life He authored for us, for we have the Word and the Spirit to strengthen, help, and guide us.

Chapter 6

Living & Walking in the Spirit

> Jesus said to me that night, "*You have called out for that place in the anointing, which God appreciates, but you must be sober about the responsibilities that anointing calls for. It pleases God to bless you with that anointing, but then it calls for you to be pleased to bring yourself in line with the responsibilities of that anointing.*
>
> "*Smith Wigglesworth is an example of the consecration and responsibility toward that anointing. He lived and walked in the Spirit with ease, freedom, and liberty as he spent his days in feeding and meditation on the Word and in fellowship with God through his ongoing devoted prayer life. Be mindful and purposeful to give yourself to the lifestyle of intake of the Word and fellowship with Me through continued prayer.*"

Smith Wigglesworth was a minister from England whose ministry was in the forefront during the first half of the 1900s. He was a man of bold faith who was known as being a man of the Word and the Spirit.

He owned his own plumbing business until his mid 50s, then God called him into the full-time ministry. During his ministry, he traveled all over the world and saw multitudes healed, and there were several accounts of people being raised from the dead under his ministry.

Even during his years as a plumber, many people were healed, and a few people were raised from the dead. Being in business didn't keep him from developing his spiritual life. His walk with God was strong and fruitful because feeding on the Word and fellowshipping with God in prayer was a flow of his daily life.

I have always greatly appreciated and studied about Smith Wigglesworth through the years, so when Jesus pointed to him as an example to follow, I had a clear understanding of what Jesus was referring to.

Jesus said to me regarding Smith Wigglesworth, *"He lived and walked in the Spirit with ease, freedom, and liberty...."*

How was Smith Wigglesworth able to live and walk in the Spirit with ease, freedom, and liberty? The next phrase Jesus spoke to me tells us how. *"...As he spent his days in feeding and meditation on the Word and in fellowship with God through his ongoing devoted prayer life."* He lived full of the Word and the Spirit.

Carrying On in the Anointing

When Jesus said to me that night, *"You have called out for that place in the anointing...and it pleases God to bless you with that anointing...,"* I knew He was referring to the "Double Portion" Anointing.

However, I couldn't specifically remember ever asking for or talking to God about receiving a double portion of the anointing that was on my husband when he went to Heaven in 2013. But when he went to Heaven, I knew that there was no part of the ministry that would be stopped or changed. We were continuing on as we did when he was here.

Through the years, my husband had ministered to me on several occasions about being called to the same office he occupied, so when he went to Heaven, I was able to continue with the role that he had fulfilled in the ministry. Yes, there are differences between how he flowed and how I flow in that office, but the work of it is still being carried on. In that respect, nothing changed upon his departure – we carried on as before.

When he was here, the two of us were moving together in carrying out the work, but upon his departure, I carried on with what we had both walked in. Even though I don't recall asking for a double portion, I refused to back up, and I continued on. Possibly it was my actions of continuing that put a demand on it and helped qualify me to receive that degree of anointing.

In addition, I had been talking about and believing for what my husband spoke by the Spirit – that the Last Days Revival would see the fivefold offices and the nine gifts of the Spirit operating at their full potential power. It came to me that believing and calling in prayer for that to come to pass in the Body of Christ was me calling for the "Double Portion" Anointing without realizing it.

Responsibilities of the Anointing

When Jesus spoke of being sober about the responsibilities that the anointing calls for, He immediately followed that up by speaking of the spiritual life of Smith Wigglesworth – how he lived and walked in the Spirit through his life in the Word and in prayer. *Living and walking in the Spirit is the primary way to walk responsibly toward the anointing.*

The responsibilities that the anointing calls for lie first and foremost with us developing and tending to our fellowship with God through the Word and prayer. Our fellowship with God is the fountain out of which all the blessings in our life and ministry flow.

It is our glorious privilege and responsibility to live full of the Word and the Spirit and to know God so that others may know Him, too. It is not a hard labor or responsibility, but a joy that can be carried out as Smith Wigglesworth did, "...with ease, freedom, and liberty...."

One man who worked closely with Kathryn Kuhlman said about her, "Kathryn Kuhlman was so consecrated and dedicated to God that her life made it easy for others to receive what they needed from God."

Throughout his life and ministry, the Apostle Paul saw many healings, miracles, and dramatic events take place, but even after having seen all those things, he states his great longing, *"That I may know him, and the power of his resurrection..."* (Phil. 3:10).

Seeing great miracles, healings, and dramatic events could never substitute for knowing Him. Paul still longed to know Jesus more and more – and to know the power outflowing from His resurrection that belongs to the believer.

Our lives have been changed and affected the most by those who have known God.

Years ago, as I was examining my devotional life, the Spirit of God spoke the following to me:

> *Don't relegate your devotional life to a time of day. Your devotion to Him* ***is*** *your day – devoted to Him in your thoughts, your actions, in the motives of your heart, what you do with your body, how you handle your money, and devoted to Him with your time. Don't get caught in the mental trap of clocking your time with Him. But your devotion to Him is to be carried out as you start every day in the Spirit; then keep your heart turned toward Him all day long.*
>
> *Take advantage of every free moment of the day to feed on His Word, meditate on the Word, talk to Him in prayer, and edify yourself through speaking in tongues. Your devotional time is not to be only set for a certain time, but woven throughout the moments of your day, and responding immediately to every*

prompting of the Spirit that leads you to pray or toward the Word.

*God is not trying to bring you into **times** in the Spirit, but into a **life** in the Spirit.*

Anything different than this will be mental planning and human effort, and it will take the life out of your fellowship with God, for the letter of the law kills, but the Spirit gives life.

Chapter 7

My Yoke Is Light & Easy

That night, Jesus said to me, *"My yoke is light and easy. This* (living in the Spirit and walking responsibly toward the anointing) *can be accomplished with lightness and ease as you give yourself to focusing on these two things – continually feeding and meditating on the Word, and continual prayer and fellowship with God. Doing these two things will help you keep the door closed to the mind and the flesh, through which Satan and his strategies gain entrance.*

"Meditate often and much on the lightness and the ease of My yoke, that you think right toward these things."

What is His yoke? His will and His plan for our lives, which is to be carried out His way – by living and walking in the Spirit. His yoke is light and easy. If life becomes difficult and hard, we are yoking up with the wrong things and the wrong flow. Stay yoked up with Jesus – God's will being carried out His way.

We stay under the right yoke and the right flow as we have a daily lifestyle of feeding and meditating on the Word and praying and fellowshipping with God.

Through the Word and prayer, our spirits are strengthened and fortified to take the lead in our lives, dominating over our minds and bodies.

The strategies of the enemy gain entrance into our lives through the mental and physical arenas. The mental arena is Satan's arena. He seeks to hold us in the mental arena, the thinking arena, for he is masterful in that arena – he can out-think us. But we are to hold him in the spirit arena, the arena of faith, for in that arena we are master.

Our lives are not to be led by our minds and our bodies, which gives the enemy a place of entrance into our lives, but rather be led and dominated by our spirits.

For those who find themselves struggling with things of the mind and flesh, giving the Word and prayer first place in their lives is the remedy. This will enable them to live and move under the light and easy flow of Jesus' yoke.

As we give the Word first place, and as we fellowship with God in prayer, we are enabled to live and walk in the Spirit, and it's by walking in the Spirit that we are able to meet the responsibilities of the anointing upon our lives, As we live in the Spirit, we stay in the flow of that which is light and easy, where opposition, hindrances, and challenges are easily overcome.

The Right Flow of Peace & Joy

Why did Jesus say to meditate often and much on the lightness and the ease of His yoke? We must think right toward His plan, think right about our calls, our ministries, and all that we do for the Lord, so that we don't begin to view it as heavy or as a hardship that makes life difficult.

It is a complete joy and privilege to be a co-laborer with God. His plan for our lives gives us a purpose worth living for and gives us the best life. The enemy would love for us to think wrong toward these things, for wrong thinking is an open door to him.

Romans 14:17 & 18 tells us, *"For the kingdom of God is not meat and drink; but righteousness, and peace, and joy in the Holy Ghost. For he that in these things serveth Christ is acceptable to God, and approved of men."*

The Kingdom of God is righteousness, peace, and joy in the Holy Ghost. This is the flow of the Holy Ghost. If we are in the flow of the Holy Ghost, we are walking daily in peace and joy. If we have left walking in peace and joy, we have left the flow of the Holy Ghost.

Verse 18 in the Amplified translation reads, *"He who serves Christ in this way is acceptable and pleasing to God and is approved by men."*

"He who serves Christ in this way...." What way? Walking in righteousness, peace, and joy. *"He who serves Christ in this way is acceptable and pleasing to God and is approved by*

men." To serve God in this way is acceptable and pleasing to God, but to serve Him without being in joy and peace would be unacceptable to Him.

If we are not walking in peace and joy, we are walking the wrong way. If we think His plan, the ministry, and what He has called us to is heavy and burdensome, we are thinking and walking the wrong way.

Jesus told me that we are to, *"Meditate often and much on the lightness and the ease of My yoke, that you think right toward these things."*

We are to meditate often and much on the lightness and ease of His yoke, for it will keep us safeguarded from wrong thinking when faced with opposition that comes.

The hardness of this world is all around us, but He has delivered us from that flow, so although opposition comes, we don't have to let it *in* us. For those yoked up with God's will and God's plan, the flow is light and easy.

Because the hardness of the flow of this world is all around us, the mind can slip back into the natural and start thinking wrong – thinking the "hard" flow instead of the "light and easy" flow. The yoke of His plan for our lives is light and easy.

Proverbs 13:15 tells us that the way of the transgressor is hard. If things are a difficulty and a struggle, then we are yoked up with the wrong thing. It's the way of the transgressor that is hard. If things are hard, where have we transgressed from His will, from His Word, or from right thinking?

Yes, challenges and opposition will come, but as we are doers of the Word and stay in the Spirit, we can face and deal with those things in His power and ability, and they are overcome.

We must make certain we are thinking right toward that which opposes us. If opposition is troubling our minds, then we need to answer that opposition with the Word of God and bring our thinking back in line with God's Word. Opposition will come, but one of the hardest things we have to deal with is our own wrong thinking. When we think right, even difficult things are made easy. We can easily sail through great challenges when we think and speak right.

Jesus was opposed daily, but He didn't live His life with a troubled and harassed mind, struggling under the burden of what He was born for, so we must not allow ourselves to live differently than He lived.

Hebrews 1:9 tells us of Jesus, *"Thou hast loved* ***righteousness****, and hated iniquity; therefore God, even thy God, hath anointed thee with the oil of* ***gladness*** *above thy fellows."*

The degree of gladness and joy Jesus walked in was unequaled by any man. Jesus lived and walked in the flow of the Kingdom of God – He walked in righteousness, peace, and joy.

His degree of gladness and joy was so great because He loved righteousness and hated iniquity. When we obey God's plan, and when we live clean before the Lord, our gladness will be great. But those who live in disobedience or persist in a lifestyle of sin and iniquity will have troubled and harassed minds; it will rob them of joy.

How Jesus Walked

In Matthew, Jesus stated,

> **MATTHEW 11:29 & 30** ***(Amplified)***
> **29 Take My yoke upon you and learn of Me, for I am gentle (meek) and humble (lowly) in heart, and you will find rest (relief and ease and refreshment and recreation and blessed quiet) for your souls.**
> **30 For My yoke is wholesome (useful, good – not harsh, hard, sharp, or pressing, but comfortable, gracious, and pleasant), and My burden is light and easy to be borne.**

Notice the phrase, "...learn of Me...." We are to learn how He lived and conducted Himself – learn how He walked through hardness with ease.

One thing we know about how Jesus walked was that He lived full of the Spirit. Luke 4:1 reads, *"And Jesus being **full** of the Holy Ghost...was led by the Spirit...."*

Jesus accomplished God's plan by living full of the Spirit and being led of the Spirit. Since that's how He was able to fulfill and accomplish God's plan, we can't expect to fulfill God's plan any other way. Living in the Spirit is simply allowing our spirits to dominate us, rather than our minds and our bodies.

We must become skillful at living and walking in the Spirit by practicing it every day. To become skillful at anything, whether it's natural or spiritual, we have to practice.

Life in the Spirit is to be the emphasis of the New Testament believer, for in the New Testament, we are instructed to walk in the Spirit, live in the Spirit, pray in the Spirit, and sing in the Spirit.

Jesus told one minister, "The important thing is to minister in the power of the Spirit." How do we effectively *minister* in the power of the Spirit unless we also *live* in the power of the Spirit?

Living in God's Presence

> That night in Russia, Jesus went on to say to me, *"In My presence is fullness of joy. Carry out My plan in My presence, then you will hold yourself in the joy of this flow – where the mind and the body are always kept under the dominion of your spirit* (through continual intake of the Word & prayer).
>
> *"Be an example in this, for you have the help of the greater One to carry this out."*

In His presence is fullness of joy (Ps. 16:11). In His presence is where fullness is; it is where joy becomes full. Living in His presence offers us a life full of joy. To live life apart from being mindful of His presence is a life less than fullness. His best is that we all live and carry out His plan in His presence. Anything less will rob us of the best life He offers us.

A life lived in His presence is fueled by a continual intake of the Word and prayer. In His presence, our spirits are strengthened and fortified to take the lead in our lives, dominating over our minds and bodies. Struggles of the mind and flesh lose sway as we live in His presence.

Years ago, God said to me, "When you see someone succumb to sin, others will say that sin took them out. But it's not sin that took them. (Romans 6 tells us that sin no longer has dominion over us and shall not lord over us, for we have a new Lord.) If they would have started their day with Me, they would have been fortified to take their stand against sin. Their failure was in not starting their day with Me."

We can live and walk in the Spirit, no longer being dominated by the mind and the body, but it is up to us to give Him first place in our daily lives – choosing to turn and hold our attention and focus on Him – living in His presence.

Jesus states, *"Behold, I stand at the door and knock; if anyone* ***hears*** *and* ***listens to*** *and heeds My voice and* ***opens*** *the door, I will* ***come in*** *to him and will eat with him, and he [will eat] with Me"* (Rev. 3:20, Amplified). He is a perfect gentleman; He will not come in uninvited.

He enters where room is made for Him. Throughout the day, we can live in His presence as we make room for Him in our day. We make room for Him by turning our attention and focus toward Him and away from everything else so that we may fellowship with Him and hear what He would say to us.

As we draw nigh unto Him, He will respond by drawing nigh to us (James 4:8). The move is ours to make – He will meet our movement toward Him.

Psalm 91:1 invites us, *"He that dwelleth in the secret place of the most High shall abide under the shadow of the Almighty."* The secret place is "in the Spirit," the place of His presence. We're not only invited to visit there, but to abide there.

As we abide in and occupy that place in the Spirit, we are to also go further in the Spirit. As we do, we must then *protect* that place in the Spirit by not allowing the natural and the unimportant to distract us or draw us away from that place.

Taking Up Our Cross Lifts Us

> That night, Jesus said to me, *"There is no burden to the responsibilities of the anointing – as you take up your cross to follow Me, it* ***lifts*** *you into the lightness and ease of* ***My*** *flow. I never conducted My earthly life as being under a burden of the price I was to pay. Life for Me was a great joy and delight. I only experienced being a Man of sorrows and acquainted with grief for a few brief moments on the cross. But I carried sorrows and griefs so that you would never experience it for a moment. In bearing it, I freed you*

> *from it so that you would only live your life under that which is light and easy.*
>
> *"You need this to accomplish the fullness of My will. Now, move in it, and you will be lifted above that which tries to trouble you. As you walk daily in this direction, you will see difficulties and challenges fall off you."*

Jesus lived His life in His Father's presence. He lived mindful that His Father was ever-present – His attention was held there. He lived mindful that it was the Father in Him that was doing the works. *"...but the Father that dwelleth in me, he doeth the works"* (John 14:10). Jesus wore His responsibilities lightly – they were not a burden to Him, for in the Father's presence, everything is light.

What a lightness, what an ease that means for us when we realize that the works are the Father's responsibility. Our responsibility is simply to live in His presence, follow and obey His plan, and allow Him to flow through us unhindered.

In His presence is fullness of joy. The joy that flows in His presence inoculates us against the many joyless circumstances that arise around us, and it makes us immune to the burden those joyless circumstances try to place on us – they cannot attach themselves to us.

"Thou wilt shew me the path of life: in thy presence is fulness of joy; at thy right hand there are pleasures for evermore" (Ps. 16:11). Notice the first phrase: *"Thou wilt shew me the path of life...."* What is the path of life? The next phrase tells us: *"...in thy presence is fulness of joy...."*

What a life this gives us! A life full of joy that comes from living in His presence! No burdens, no heaviness. Yes, we have responsibilities in this life, but as we live in His presence, He does the work. *"...But the Father that dwelleth in me, he doeth the works."* We do the "work" of living in His presence, and as we live in His presence, His directions for us become clear; we obey His directions, and the work is done. What a life!

God's will and plan can only be carried out to its fullest as we live in His presence, walking in the Spirit and following His leadings; that's how we stay in that which is light and easy. His will and plan is never grievous or burdensome, so if what we're doing seems heavy, troublesome, and a burden, then we're doing it wrong – we have left the highest flow He made available to us. We are to again turn our attention and focus back to Him and walk in the Spirit.

His plan is to be carried out in His presence. Jesus was our example in this. He stated that He only did what He saw His Father do. He only said what He heard His Father say. It was in His Father's presence that He would see and hear what He needed for the day.

It is no different for us. As we live in His presence, giving ourselves time in the Spirit, we can see and hear from our Father what we need for our lives and ministries.

In His presence, we gain clarity for what's ahead and for decisions we must make. We are not to make decisions apart from Him. We are not to move too fast, not move until we have the needed clarity that we gain in His presence.

That which tries to trouble or hinder us has no place to stand in His presence, so those things begin to fall off and away from our lives as we continue to live in His presence. We are not to just *begin* to move in this, but *continue* to move in these things so that we can continually live above the difficulties and challenges that arise.

Jesus was an example in this for us, and we are to be an example in this for others.

Chapter 8

Part 2 – Additional Things God Said

The morning after Jesus spoke to me, God spoke to me further by the Spirit and gave the following points He wanted me to expound on. (The following chapters are teaching on each of these points.)

To walk in the "Double Portion" Anointing:

1. It calls for great wisdom, great consecration, great discipline of the spirit over the mind and body, and great accuracy. (I will deal with each one of these in their own separate chapters.)
2. It calls for maturity of consecration. It calls for a "John the Baptist" consecration – living apart with God so you can hear Him – living away from distractions of the natural life.
3. The pioneers of great faith walked in the "Double Portion" Anointing. It is available to those who are faithful to another man, as Elisha was to Elijah. (You can't just get in a ministry line and have hands laid on you to receive this.)

4. It calls for great skill with the anointing and with the call that's entrusted to you.
5. The greater the anointing, the smaller the margin for error.
6. It demands right fellowship and protecting right connections to divine supplies in your life.
7. It calls for great renewing of the mind. (An unrenewed area of the mind is the entrance place of defeat.)
8. I only say what I hear My Father say. I only do what I see My Father do. (It calls for keen and accurate hearing and seeing, and great discipline to hold the thoughts, mouth, and actions to what is seen and heard from the Father.)
9. "Double Portion" Anointing is not a place to be feared, but a place to be sober about – great soberness.
10. To walk in this does not call for a perfect man (without flaws), but for a perfectly- surrendered man.

Chapter 9

Great Wisdom

God said to me in Russia, *"To walk in the 'Double Portion' Anointing calls for great wisdom."*

PROVERBS 4:6-8 *(Amplified)*
6 Forsake not [Wisdom], and she will KEEP, DEFEND, and PROTECT you; love her, and she will GUARD you.
7 The beginning of Wisdom is: get Wisdom (skillful and godly Wisdom)! [For skillful and godly Wisdom is the principal thing.] And with all you have gotten, get understanding (discernment, comprehension, and interpretation).
8 Prize Wisdom highly and exalt her, and she will exalt and promote you; she will bring you to honor when you embrace her.

We need the wisdom of God to be promoted into all that God has for us. We need wisdom to accomplish what we are born for and to fulfill the will and call of God on our lives.

When you carry an anointing, you become a target for the enemy, and it takes walking in wisdom to not fall into his traps. The greater the anointing you walk in, the bigger the target you become, so the greater degree of wisdom you must walk in – in every arena – spiritually, mentally, physically, and materially.

In the passage above, verse 6 tells us that as we walk in wisdom, it will keep, defend, protect, and guard us. That's why we must highly prize wisdom (vs. 8).

When walking in a great anointing, we must prize wisdom as much as we prize the anointing, because wisdom helps us to walk successfully in that anointing.

The further I go in this life, the more I value and prize wisdom, for the greater the wisdom I walk in, the better and easier life becomes.

Ignorance makes life hard. It robs from us – it robs us from living the best life.

The devil thrives on ignorance. He is counting on people's ignorance to work his plan in their lives.

The devil works through ignorance, but not God – God only works through knowledge. God can't work through ignorance, for He has no association with it.

Hosea 4:6 tells us, *"My people are destroyed for lack of knowledge...."* In this verse, the devil is not even mentioned. God's people aren't destroyed because of the enemy, for Colossians 2:15 tells us that Jesus spoiled and defeated the enemy; He defeated him on our behalf and handed us the victory. It's not the devil, but lack of knowledge that destroys

God's people. Lack of knowledge is dangerous. The word "destroyed" means cut off. God's people are cut off from the blessings of God that belong to them because of ignorance.

The Word is the cure for ignorance. When we renew our minds, walking in the light God's Word gives, ignorance is run out of our lives, thereby closing the door to the enemy, refusing him entrance into our lives.

Wisdom is walking in and rightly applying the knowledge God's Word gives.

Nothing can take the place of wisdom. As important as faith is, even faith can't take the place of wisdom in our lives. No other spiritual quality or spiritual force can substitute for wisdom and the blessing it gives.

Deuteronomy 34:9 tells us, *"And Joshua the son of Nun was full of the spirit of wisdom; for Moses had laid his hands upon him...."* When Moses laid hands on Joshua, a spirit of wisdom came into Joshua, and he was able to lead God's people into the land God had for them. Wisdom helps us to move into what God has for us.

When Solomon asked, he was given the wisdom he needed to be king. To lead successfully, we need the wisdom of God.

Luke 2:40 records about Jesus, *"And the child grew, and waxed strong in spirit, **filled with wisdom**: and the grace of God was upon him."* Luke 2:52 states, *"And Jesus **increased in wisdom** and stature, and in favour with God and man."*

Jesus was the Son of God, but that didn't dismiss Him from the need to walk in wisdom. The anointing is no substitute for wisdom; they each have their place. For Jesus to walk successfully under the anointing that would come upon Him when He was baptized by John the Baptist, He would need to be filled with wisdom.

The greater the anointing, the greater the degree of wisdom that is needed. We must grow in wisdom.

Wisdom in Every Arena of Life

As Jesus said to me, to walk in the "Double Portion" Anointing calls for great wisdom. That would include wisdom in every arena of life – spiritually, mentally, physically, and materially. Let's look at wisdom in these arenas, as well as a few other areas.

Wisdom in the Spiritual Arena – Walking in the Will of God

"Jesus saith unto them, My meat is to do the will of him that sent me, and to finish his work" (John 4:34). That which nourished Jesus' life was to do the will of God.

With all the opposition Jesus faced, nothing could touch Him because staying in God's will made Him untouchable. He couldn't even be crucified until He laid down His own life – no man took His life from Him – He laid it down to fulfill the will of God. Walking in God's will made Him master over all that came against Him.

Ephesians 2:10 tells us, *"...[**taking paths which He prepared** ahead of time], **that we should walk in them [living the good life** which He prearranged and made ready for us to live]"* (Amplified). To live "the good life," we must take the "paths which He prepared" for us. To veer from the paths He prepared is to veer from the good life.

All the blessings of God are connected to His will and plan for our lives. Long life, health, prosperity, peace, joy, victory, and all His blessings are connected to His plan. To veer from His plan is to veer from the fullness of these blessings and His best.

We need wisdom to understand His will for our lives. Ephesians 5:17 instructs us, *"Wherefore be ye not unwise, but understanding what the will of the Lord is."* To not understand what the will of God is for our lives is unwise – a lack of wisdom.

Wisdom in the Mental Arena

Wisdom in the mental arena includes the renewing of the mind. A renewed mind is a disciplined mind, and a disciplined mind is a renewed mind.

To walk in wisdom, we must put good mental habits in place – we must discipline and guard our thought lives, paying attention to what we allow ourselves to think on. A disciplined mind doesn't allow itself to entertain or touch certain things in the thought life.

Entertaining thoughts of fear, worry, complaining, griping, offense, unforgiveness, ill will toward others, bitterness, strife, and all "like" things are a bad mental habit and point to an unrenewed, undisciplined mind.

If someone is struggling with any of these things, that lets them know what they need to focus on in the renewing of their mind.

Yes, it is a full-time job to pay attention to and to discipline the thought life, but we can become skillful at it. The more we renew our minds with God's Word, the easier it becomes.

The mental arena is Satan's arena. He tries to draw us into the mental arena through threats, suggestions, and bombarding thoughts, for he knows if he can get us in the mental arena, he can whip us. But we are to hold him in the spirit arena – the arena of faith – and when we do, we will whip him, and whip him badly.

We are to recognize his strategy of trying to draw us in the mental arena and become skillful at not yielding to his strategy. We are to stay in the spirit arena – the faith arena – by answering each of his threats and suggestions with the Word of God, and then by beginning to praise God. Praising God helps hold us in the spirit arena and keeps us from drifting back into the mental arena.

The further we progress in the anointing, the more disciplined we must become in our thought lives. There are certain things we cannot allow ourselves to entertain or even touch in our thought life, or we will open the door to the devil.

Wisdom calls for us to be watchful and vigilant at all times – slothful and slack in nothing, but diligent and disciplined in our thought lives.

Second Corinthians 10:5 instructs us, *"Casting down imaginations, and every high thing that exalteth itself against the knowledge of God, and bringing into captivity* ***every thought*** *to the obedience of Christ."*

Wisdom in the Physical Arena

In the life of Solomon, we see some vital truths. When Solomon asked God for an understanding heart so he could judge and lead the people, God told him He had given him a wise and understanding heart. But because his request pleased God, He had also given him what he didn't ask for – riches and honor. Then He told him, *"And if thou wilt walk in my ways, to keep my statutes and my commandments, as thy father David did walk, then I will lengthen thy days"* (1 Kings 3:14).

Notice that having long life is conditional. It's connected to keeping God's statues and commandments (vs.14). In other words, to enjoy long life, we must be doers of the Word.

We can see from what God told Solomon that prosperity, honor, and long life are connected to wisdom.

Custodians of Our Bodies

We must walk in wisdom toward our physical bodies and have proper regard for natural laws and also for diet, exercise, and rest. We can't violate laws of nature and think it won't affect us.

When a man asked one minister toward the end of his life if there was anything he would have done differently, without hesitation, he said he would have taken better care of his body.

Our bodies are our greatest assets because our bodies house our spirits. For our spirits to stay on the earth, they need a body. Therefore, we must take care of our bodies, for we are the custodians of our bodies – not God.

By not taking proper care of our bodies, we can open the door to sickness and disease.

Diet & Exercise:

Regarding our diet and exercise, we must walk in wisdom; each person must find the way of eating and the exercise that works best for them. We can follow good sense and science. We need to use good sense, and also if something is shown scientifically to be good for us or not to be good for us, we need to pay attention to that. However, with all the information that's out there today, I realize it's not always easy to know which report is right, but find what suits you and your body best.

To help with our diet and exercise, we must discipline our thought lives and govern our mouths. Some say, "I hate to exercise. I can't lose weight." Those words are working against you. Instead, make your words work for you.

With our diet and exercise, we can draw on divine help. Find scriptures that encourage you and meditate on them and confess them over yourself. Also, take time to pray in tongues a few minutes before meals, which builds up your spirit so that you are able to control your flesh. You can govern your diet and exercise with the help of the Spirit.

Have you ever noticed how you get stirred up to eat better and exercise when you read or watch something about it, but after a few days, you're not so stirred up about it anymore? Years ago, God said to me, "Faith comes by hearing, but faith for everything comes by hearing. So every day, read or watch something regarding diet and exercise, and it will keep you stirred up to help you do it."

Discipline in our diet is something that we always have to pay attention to. One minister used to have two days a week that he fasted, then God spoke to him and said, "I would be more pleased if you lived a fasted life rather than just had days of fasting. That is, never eat all your body wants." He was basically telling him to always be moderate in his eating and not excessive.

Because the Bible doesn't give strict guidelines for diet, we are not to take our personal convictions about diet and preach them as doctrine for others to live by. One minister told of having seen preachers exchange their message of Jesus the Healer for sermons on dieting, and they lost the anointing. We are to stay balanced and not get into a ditch.

Don't think that a diet can do for you what only Jesus' stripes did for you. If a diet needs to be adjusted for some physical things to change in your body, then make that adjustment. But through the years, I have seen people go to the extreme and think that their diet can do for them what only Jesus' healing power can accomplish. They began putting more faith in their diet than in the healing power of God.

We also have to make certain we don't become fear-motivated with our diet. One man asked my husband to come and pray for a relative who was dying in the hospital. We had known of this person and had heard how rigid they were in their diet regime – they were excessive. But they became entrenched in their diet and supplement regime out of fear of getting certain diseases. In the process, they had shifted their faith from the healing Word and a healing Jesus to "healing foods" and supplements. Don't do anything out of fear, for fear is an open door to the enemy.

When Ed went into their hospital room to pray for them, God told him, "They're going to die because they have more faith in their diet and supplements than they do in the stripes of Jesus."

When someone shifts their faith from the healing Word to healing foods, they're trying to take their health into their own hands. Yes, we are the custodians of our bodies. Yes, we should do right toward our diets. But that is no substitute for the power of God.

Every day, we need His power! We need His healing power. We need His keeping power. We need His miracle power. We live by His power. Our faith is to be in the power of God.

Yes, we need to change any bad eating habits, especially if God deals specifically with us about it. But don't try to take control of your health with only natural means, for a diet is no substitute for the stripes Jesus took for us to have healing and divine health.

To walk in divine health required a divine sacrifice – the stripes of Jesus. Diet can never do for anyone what only His stripes and His power can do.

Rest:

If the devil can't stop you from going forward, then he'll try to drive you from behind – driving and pushing you so you don't rest properly. God leads, He never drives.

Many think they're being lazy if they take time to rest, but the enemy can energize that way of thinking so that they can become driven to keep working. Then without proper rest, their bodies become broken down and they get taken out of their race prematurely.

Mark 6:7 tells of Jesus sending the disciples out to minister with authority and power, and when they returned, He said to them, *"...come away by yourselves to a deserted place, and rest a while..."* (Mark 6:31, Amplified).

Jesus was training them that after a time of ministry they were to go to a place away from people so they could rest for a while – not just for a day, but for a while. He would not have instructed them to do something He didn't do Himself.

Because we are still human with mortal bodies, we need to rest appropriately.

On the seventh day of Creation, the Word tells us that God rested; He set the example for us to follow. We can't dismiss His example and think that our lives won't be affected by it.

Different people need different amounts of rest to function at their best, so everyone needs to know how much rest they need to live rested.

Not resting properly is a bad habit of the flesh that must be dealt with. When younger, people may get by with that bad habit, but as they get older, it will catch up with them.

I remember hearing one woman refer to her father who was a leading minister in a past revival. She spoke of seeing the number of hours he worked every day and thought he was the most disciplined man she had ever seen. But after he died prematurely, she realized that what he really had was a lack of discipline because he didn't properly rest.

The mindset of many ministers of the past who died prematurely was seen in the statement, "I'd rather burn out than rust out." But we don't have to burn out or rust out. We can live out our lives on the earth, and when we're satisfied, go to Heaven without sickness and disease.

I know how much rest I need to function at my best, so I schedule rest days into my calendar just like I schedule preaching dates. I rest one day a week, but after several weeks, I take a few days together to rest because it takes time just for the anointing to lift off of me so that I can rest properly.

Because I travel so much in the ministry, it is very physically demanding, so I have to make sure I get proper rest. I refuse to not enjoy the race I'm running, so I refuse to live tired.

If a traveling minister is tired all the time, he will end up not enjoying the constant travel and be tempted to complain against his call, which is dangerous for any minister. If living tired, he can be tempted to not travel as he should, to entertain settling down, or to stop traveling and start a church, which can get him in trouble with God if God isn't in it.

Many people, even ministers, lose the joy of fulfilling what they're born for because they fail to rest. When living tired, things are not as enjoyable as they should be, but we must guard against that because fulfilling the plan of God for our lives is not only a great honor, but it is to be a great joy. Let's not sabotage ourselves in the joyful way we are to run our race by living tired.

The Lord is the strength of our lives, and as we use our faith, God's strength will enable us to accomplish more, but His strength is not meant to substitute for resting our bodies properly.

Any world-class athlete knows that winning doesn't just happen because they're the best in their sport. There are other factors involved – proper training, right mental attitude, diet, but also proper rest.

Proper rest is a much over-looked requirement of running our race accurately and joyfully.

It's difficult to yield to the Spirit when we're tired. When we are tired, we are not as keen as we should be, which could result in us missing or failing to recognize leadings of the Spirit, which can get us into trouble and ultimately end up affecting and hindering our spiritual lives.

Living tired could also result in us making poor decisions, especially if we are not as keen as we should be to the leadings of the Spirit.

Not only that, but when we're overly tired, we can become less watchful against the strategies of the enemy, and thereby give place to the enemy.

Rest & the Anointing

As believers, we have an anointing that abides *within* that we can draw on for our daily lives. But those who stand in a fivefold office have an anointing that comes *upon* that enables them to minister to the people.

Based on which office someone stands in, the anointing that comes upon can have a different effect on the body. For some, the anointing energizes them, but for those ministers who operate under a *tangible* anointing, it is weighty and can drain the body of strength.

In this revival of the last days, when the fivefold offices and the nine gifts of the Spirit are operating at 100% of their potential power, our bodies must be fit to operate under that degree of power and under the weightiness of that anointing. Proper rest will be even more important then, so we must discipline ourselves in it.

As one seasoned minister stated, "It's the anointing that strengthens and empowers us to teach, preach, and heal. Don't make ministry decisions under that anointing because that's not what the anointing is for. The anointing is to empower us to teach, preach, and heal. Don't mistake the strength of the anointing for energy, which the body needs through proper rest."

Some ministers conduct many services a week, so that anointing continues to stay on them day after day, and they may feel strong. But when that anointing does lift off them, they feel how tired their bodies really are, so they think the thing to do is to get back under that anointing so they can again feel strengthened. They are trying to live off the anointing. That's not what that ministry anointing is for; it is not a substitute for proper rest. If those ministers don't learn to come out from under the anointing long enough to rest, over time, they will start having problems with their bodies.

I was talking to a seasoned minister who had just finished conducting a crusade. He said that after a series of meetings, he has to go away to rest because if he doesn't, he ends up staying in the stream, and the stream keeps flowing. I understood what he meant by that. He was simply saying that if he stays around the ministry, the anointing on him will keep flowing; he has to go aside so he can come out from under the flow of that anointing and get proper rest.

That's in keeping with what Jesus said to the disciples upon their return from their ministry trip. *"...**Come away** by yourselves to a deserted place, and **rest a while**..."* (Mark 6:31, Amplified).

Ministers can't rest when they stay around the needs of the people, for their needs will make a draw on the anointing that's on them; that anointing will keep flowing, and the minister won't be able to rest properly. Notice in this scripture that Jesus said to "rest a while." It takes more than one day to fully rest – it can take "a while."

Balance

Now, there must be balance to this as well. Some don't have a strong work ethic and will use rest as an excuse to be irresponsible toward working. They must discipline their flesh and guard against laziness.

Some have a habit of complaining, saying they are overworked so they don't have time to rest. But I like what one minister said. "You're not overworked, you're unorganized!" Being properly organized will give you time to rest properly, for when you're organized, you don't take on tasks and activities that distract from what is important.

That same minister went on to state, "Work doesn't kill people, lack of rest does."

To walk in great wisdom includes giving our bodies proper rest.

We are to draw on the strength and grace God gives, then we will be strengthened to carry out the plan of God for our lives and produce much fruit. As we live and walk in the Spirit, He will enable us to produce multiplied results in a fraction of the time with less effort.

Our calls never rob from us, but lack of wisdom will.

To walk under the anointing God has for us calls for us to walk in great wisdom.

Wisdom in the Material & Financial Arena

There is much that could be said about wisdom in the material and financial arena, but I will just touch on a few things.

We must continually renew our minds with the Word regarding the prosperity that belongs to us so we don't slip into wrong thinking toward money. We must feed our faith in this arena because money issues are really faith issues.

If we think wrong about money, we will believe wrong, and if we believe wrong, we will speak wrong and be hindered in receiving what we need.

If we talk about the lack of money, it will keep it from coming in. Instead, we are to talk about how God is taking care of us and supplying our needs.

God Is Our Provider

Our prosperity lies with the will and plan of God. God's will is our wealthy place.

Isaiah 1:19 reads, *"If ye be willing and obedient, ye shall eat the good of the land."* As long as we are obedient to His will and His plan and carry it out willingly and joyfully, then we are in position for His abundance to reach our lives.

As a traveling minister, it's not road meetings that meet my needs, rather it's obeying God in going where He tells me to go. There are times He has instructed me to travel much, and times He told me not to travel much. He wanted to prove to me that road meetings are not my provider – He is – so I obey Him.

If traveling ministers think road meetings are their supply, they will try to promote their own ministry, or they will overbook themselves and wear themselves out.

If pastors think their congregation is their supply, then they won't preach all God tells them to say for fear of people leaving and losing their tithe. I've told my financial office not to tell me who in the congregation gives large offerings because I want to still say whatever I need to say to someone to rescue them, regardless of how much they may give.

Led by the Spirit, Not by Price

Before making moves, including business or financial moves, we are to look to our spirits to know God's leading. For faith to work, we must have the leading of the Spirit.

When the Spirit leads us to do something, we are to do it, no matter what finances we may or may not have. We are to go as far as we can in the natural, and the money will come.

We are to be led by the Spirit, not by money and not by price. Many have missed the will of God because they didn't want to pay a certain price. Money is a tool that is to serve us. Money is to help us fulfill the plan. We are not to hold back on the plan trying to save money; we are to use money to fulfill the plan.

If God tells me to do something, I will pay whatever I need to pay to fulfill the plan. Money is a tool to help me accomplish God's plan. I don't wait for money to give me permission to obey God. If God tells me to do something, then I go that direction; I call the money to come, and it comes.

We never had the money to do anything God told my husband and I to do, but we had the faith – so we did it. We just started moving by faith, and the money would meet our faith.

Follow Peace

We are to be careful not to move too fast and get ahead of God or miss God, but move only when we have clarity.

We may not hear God speak to us about a situation, but we may have peace about going a particular direction or making a certain decision. Once we sense peace, then we know what to do, for the peace is the clarity we need. We are always safe in following peace.

Romans 8:14 tells us that the sons of God are led by the Spirit of God. Isaiah 55:12 tells us that we are led forth with peace. The Spirit of God leads us through the peace in our spirits. When we have peace about something in our spirits, no matter what opposition may come against our minds, we are safe in following peace. If we have peace in our spirits about doing something, we are to do it. Without that peace, we are not to do it.

Wisdom Is Connected to Prosperity

In 1 Kings 3:12 & 13, God told Solomon He had given him a wise and understanding heart, but that He had also given him riches and honor, and if he would keep God's statues and commandments, he would also have long life. Notice that wisdom is connected to prosperity, honor, and long life.

To handle prosperity rightly calls for wisdom. So when people are believing God to prosper, they must also grow in wisdom to be able to handle prosperity.

Wisdom in Ministry

One aspect I particularly want to address is the vision God gives us for our ministries. The vision comes directly from God to the man of God. It doesn't come from other ministers, family members, or staff members.

When God gives the vision for a ministry, that vision must be closely guarded so that it is carried out accurately. If we veer from the God-given vision, our ministries won't produce the fruit they could. Therefore, we must protect the vision so it's not added to or subtracted from.

God does not expect us to carry out the vision He gives us alone; He will send others anointed to help us fulfill the work of the ministry and ministry business, but they are not to define or redefine the vision of the ministry; they are only to assist us in carrying it out.

We must protect the vision from well-meaning loved ones and staff who may try to speak into or redefine the vision. Someone may have a good idea or a method to help carry out the vision, but they are not to redefine the vision with "good ideas."

Through several decades of ministry, I have seen ministries and churches taken off course by those close to the man of God. It is the job of the leader to protect the vision and keep this from happening. Others may become displeased with him, but God still expects him to protect that vision and see to it that it is carried out accurately. In giving us the vision, God will also give us the wisdom to carry it out.

Wisdom in the Home

We are to live days of Heaven on earth, and our homes, marriages, and families are to be a part of that flow. Our lives, the lives of our children, and future generations are affected by what goes on in our homes, therefore, we must be vigilant and watchful over our homes.

When the enemy wants to weaken a minister and his ministry, he will look to attack his home, so we are to be mindful to keep the door closed to him. We must make certain that our marriages and families are strong.

For my husband and I, being married was Heaven on earth because we were renewing our minds with the Word of God.

We once watched an interview on television with a leading minister. He stated that he and his wife had to work on their marriage. I turned to my husband and stated, "I don't ever remember us having to work on our marriage. We've just worked on renewing our minds and being doers of the Word, and that has solved any potential marriage issues." It's the renewed mind that enjoys Heaven in their home.

The best thing anyone can do for their family is to follow the plan of God for their life and obey God. Sometimes, that causes your home life to look different than the home life of others, but that doesn't mean it's wrong.

My husband was called to the traveling ministry, so he was gone much of the time. I understood that when I married him. But I loved my husband enough to want him to obey

God and fulfill His plan, therefore, I didn't try to make him like other husbands. I didn't put pressure on him to be at home with me and the children when he needed to be out ministering.

I didn't put pressure on him to be home for certain holidays, birthdays, or anniversaries. He was always considerate of us toward that, but if he wasn't home on a particular day, that was never a problem because we could always celebrate the next time we were together. I valued the plan of God more than a holiday.

If my children asked why their daddy wasn't home like other daddies, I made it clear to them that he was obeying what God wanted him to do, and that's why our lives were so blessed. I never allowed them to think they were being cheated. His obedience to God blessed our home and family – it never robbed from us. It was okay that our lives looked different from other families. The best thing for any family is living out God's plan. God blessed us immeasurably for any sacrifices made, and I made sure the kids knew that.

We never had the problem with our sons that others have had. Because their dad was gone a lot, I made sure I was with them. I loved being a mom, and I wanted to be with them as much as I could; I wasn't always trying to get someone else to take my kids. Yes, I had help from others at different times, but most of the time, I kept them with me.

I was the administrator for our ministry and later began to pastor. Thankfully, I was able to take my children with me to the offices every day. I understand that not everyone gets to be with their children throughout the day, but I was grateful I had that opportunity. By keeping my kids with me, I was able to pay close attention to them.

Another reason we didn't have problems with our children is because we kept them in the local church. They were allowed to participate in other events and activities, but we taught them that the local church services were the highlight of the week and that nothing else was as important, therefore, they weren't skipping church for other activities.

Also, I closely guarded their fellowship. Just because someone was saved didn't mean they were the best fellowship for my children. Their friends had to be someone who brought out the best in them.

Paying attention to my kids, keeping them in the local church, and guarding their fellowship were keys to raising successful children.

I never allowed my children to listen to others talk about how hard it was to be a preacher's kid. I don't believe that. When others would try to make comments like that to my children, I would correct them. My children's lives were blessed and made better by being raised in the home of a preacher, not made harder. What makes life hard for children is when parents aren't in the will of God, don't have a pastor, don't know the Word, or don't do the Word.

Ministers must guard themselves and their family against wrong thinking toward the ministry. Many comment about how they and their families have had a hard time or get beat up in the ministry. It's not the fault of the ministry for any hardness, but it's the fault of carnal people. No matter what business you're in, you're going to have to deal with carnal, unlovely people. To be in the ministry and to do the work of the ministry is a great honor. The work of the ministry is the call of God for our family, and being obedient to that call has only ever blessed us.

God's will blesses my home and my family, and it has brought us into days of Heaven on earth. His will is never grievous, but it is a complete joy and has given us the best life!

Chapter 10

Consecration

The morning when God gave me these additional instructions by the Spirit regarding The Price of the "Double Portion" Anointing, He referred to consecration three different times. So I will go ahead and include instruction regarding all three references in this one chapter.

He said there must be great consecration, maturity of consecration, and a "John the Baptist" consecration.

Great Consecration

> God said to me, *"To walk in this 'Double Portion' Anointing calls for great consecration."*

A great anointing calls for great consecration. We must live consecrated lives if we are to walk in all that God has for us. We must separate ourselves from that which would hinder or hold us back in our spiritual progress.

One minister stated, "The love of the world is the barrier keeping believers out of the supernatural."

Matthew 22:14 tells us, *"For many are called, but few are chosen."* Many are called, but few are chosen because few will consecrate and separate themselves to what God has for them. It's not God who separates or consecrates us – that is something we do.

We don't consecrate or separate ourselves so that things are subtracted from us, but so we can be available to more of what God has for us. Consecration never subtracts from us, but only adds to us.

Those who struggle against the will of God for their lives or against something He is leading them to do are not as consecrated as they should be.

No one ever fulfills a plan they're not consecrated to. Consecration brings us into being "wholehearted" toward God's plan. No one ever succeeds in any endeavor they are only half-hearted toward.

Those who reach the pinnacle in their profession, their field of study, or in any endeavor are those who are wholehearted – single in purpose and intent. They are not dividing their attention, their time, their energies, and their resources in multiple directions. They have stripped back the unimportant from their lives.

Paul told Timothy, a young preacher,

1 TIMOTHY 4:12-16 *(Amplified)*
12 ...be an example (pattern) for the believers in speech, in conduct, in love, in faith, and in purity.

13 Till I come, devote yourself to [public and private] reading, to exhortation (preaching and personal appeals), and to teaching and instilling doctrine.
14 Do not neglect the gift which is in you...
15 PRACTICE and CULTIVATE and MEDITATE upon these duties; THROW YOURSELF WHOLLY INTO THEM [as your ministry], so that your progress may be evident to everybody.
16 Look well to yourself [to your own personality] and to [your] teaching; persevere in these things [hold to them], for by so doing you will save both yourself and those who hear you.

Timothy was blessed to have a man of Paul's caliber as his spiritual father, but that did not ensure Timothy's success – that was no substitute for Timothy being consecrated and wholehearted toward the call of God.

Running Our Race

Hebrews 11 tells us of the many faith heroes who ran their race and laid hold of God's plan for their lives. Then Hebrews 12 tells us that now those heroes of faith are watching as we run our race – they are interested in the fulfillment of God's plan.

We have a race to run just like they had a race to run, and we are told what to do to run that race effectively.

HEBREWS 12:1 & 2
1 Wherefore seeing we also are compassed about with so great a cloud of witnesses, let us

> **LAY ASIDE every weight, and the sin which doth so easily beset us, and let us run with patience the race that is set before us,**
> **2 Looking unto Jesus the author and finisher of our faith....**

Lay aside every weight. God isn't the One who does that – it is our job to lay aside those things that hinder us in our race.

Any competitive runner runs to win; he's not running to lose. He wants to run at his full potential, so he gets rid of anything that would hinder or slow his pace or affect his progress. He sees those weights as enemies to his success, so he gladly searches for weights to rid himself of. He knows that getting rid of weights doesn't subtract or rob from him, but helps him to lay hold of and achieve what is most important to him.

In running our race, there are things of the past that are no longer needed, so we are to lay them aside; we are to be done with using them. If we won't lay them aside, they will hinder us in our race because we don't need them. Why do people not lay things aside? Because they're not done using them. But we need to realize the things we don't need in our race and quit using them. The more we keep using them, the less likely we are to lay them aside.

The more we are willing to lay aside of the natural realm, the more we are freed up and available to lay hold of what God offers us. We are the ones who determine what we can lay hold of by what we will lay aside.

Before we take on something, we need to ask ourselves, *Is this going to help me in my race?* We are to live mindful of the race we are running so that we don't sell off our future to the unimportant.

Run With Patience

Hebrews 12:1 & 2 also tells us, *"...let us* ***run with patience*** *the race that is set before us, Looking unto Jesus the author and finisher of our faith...."* To run successfully, we are also told how to run – run with patience.

We must not become impatient and try to step into something prematurely. We must run with patience so that we move into what His plan holds for us in His timing, allowing Him to bring us into those things.

The race He has for us to run includes preparation time. Jesus prepared 30 years for three years of earthly ministry. During Jesus' day, no one was allowed to preach or teach in the Jewish synagogues until they were 30 years old, and God didn't set aside that requirement just for His Son. Instead, He used all of that time for Jesus' preparation.

The devil would have loved to drive Him to try to step into His ministry ahead of time, before His preparation was complete and before the anointing came upon Him, for then failure would have been imminent. Without being properly prepared and trained, no one succeeds.

When Jesus was born on the earth, the Word tells us that He had laid aside His mighty glory and virtue. He wasn't born with all His knowledge; He had to find Himself in the Word, just like we do. He had to learn and be trained just like we have to. Even though Jesus was the Son of God, that didn't dismiss Him from needing to be prepared for what He was born for.

Because He was patient for the first 30 years of His life to be trained and prepared, it only took Him three years to accomplish God's plan.

Preparation time is never lost time. God can only promote us to the level of our preparation. To go further, we must be prepared to go further. When we are fully prepared, it doesn't take God long to bring us into what He has for us.

Zeal Doesn't Equal Skill

Some become zealous about getting into things that God has for their lives, but without being properly prepared and trained, their zeal will only speed them into ruin.

Zeal doesn't equal skill. Zeal is no substitute for training or skill. No man succeeds without preparation and skill. Don't allow zeal to cause you to become impatient, for without patience to be trained, there is no success in ministry, regardless of your call. Being called is no substitute for being trained.

Many emphasize that they are called, but if they value their call, they must value being trained and prepared.

Through the years of ministry, we have seen many who had calls on their lives not fulfill the ministry God had for them because they wouldn't be patient and stay put long enough to be prepared and trained. They knew they were called, but they didn't value being trained.

A call is no substitute for training. Being called doesn't qualify anyone for success – they must be trained.

Because of lack of training, knowledge, and skill, many struggle year after year in ministry, even though they're called. Having a call doesn't qualify you. You have to qualify yourself by being trained and being a good, faithful, teachable student of someone who knows God better than you.

Many are counting on their call or on the anointing to do for them what only knowledge and skill can do for them.

We must consecrate ourselves so we can run the race He authored for us, but we must also consecrate ourselves to run it His way – with patience.

Taking Paths He Prepared

Ephesians 2:10 tells us, *"...[taking paths which He prepared ahead of time], that we should walk in them [living the good life which He prearranged and made ready for us to live]"* (Amplified).

If we run our race according to God's will and plan, that means we take the paths He prepared for us. All along the paths of His plan is all the provision we will need to reach the finish line – revelation, anointing, promotion, increase, supply, health, joy, peace, and everything else He provides. As we stay with His plan, our paths are full of provision, but if we veer from His plan into our own plan, we veer from the supply and fullness His plan holds.

We have a race to run, but let us make sure we are running it according to His plan. Being consecrated to God's plan is a key ingredient to the success of our race.

Maturity of Consecration

Throughout our lives, as we develop and mature spiritually, we will come into different seasons. Each season holds its own blessings and responsibilities, and one of those responsibilities is greater consecration. Every new season and level calls for another level of consecration. With each new season, we are to meet *God's* definition of consecration, not our own definition.

As we mature into a new season, so must our consecration. The level of consecration is to increase as our maturity increases. What was perfectly acceptable for our lives in a previous season is not acceptable in the next season. It's not that we weren't consecrated in previous seasons, but further levels call for further consecration.

If a new level calls for us to lay something aside, it is because it will hinder us, slow our progress in our race, and may even be an open door to the enemy in some way.

I believe this is what was meant when God spoke to me in Russia the morning after Jesus came into my room, saying, *"The 'Double Portion' Anointing calls for maturity of consecration."*

It's not just something wrong or sinful things that hinder us in our race, but it's being distracted with the unimportant. The unimportant will rob us of our future and our destiny if we don't recognize it as unimportant. That's why Paul prayed, *"...That you may surely learn to sense what is vital, and approve and prize what is excellent and of real value [recognizing the highest and the best, and distinguishing the moral differences]..."* (Phil. 1:10, Amplified). This is a prayer about consecration.

Smith Wigglesworth stated, "Every new revelation calls for a fresh dedication." The more revelation or light of the Word we get, the more we must make changes to walk in that light.

Change is not a negative thing, for we are changed from glory to glory – on the other side of change is more glory. Greater consecration brings us into greater glory.

"John the Baptist" Consecration

John the Baptist lived his life differently than others because he was called to something different than others. He couldn't live his life like others and accomplish what he was called to. He lived in the wilderness – he lived in a place where he could hear God.

When God spoke to me in Russia and said, "The 'Double Portion' Anointing calls for a 'John the Baptist' consecration," I understood that to mean that the "Double Portion" Anointing calls for one to live in such a way that they can hear God –

shutting out the distractions of the natural life as much as possible.

This place of consecration is not a hardship for one who's under this anointing, rather it's something he longs for and seeks to do. He is not separating himself to afflict himself, but because this is the only thing that holds his interest.

No, I'm not saying that God is calling us to live as recluses, but I am saying that John the Baptist knew what he needed to do to fulfill his call.

What that means and looks like may look differently for different people. And don't misunderstand or become unbalanced in this either. Consecration doesn't mean neglecting other responsibilities. That's not consecration, that's negligence.

As God directs us into greater consecration, it is not a radical, harsh, abrupt, hard change. Just as maturing physically is gradual, we are led into a maturing of consecration the same way we come into maturing physically – it's a process.

Kathryn Kuhlman stated to a minister close to her that she couldn't live her life like other women. In conducting crusades, she had to prepare herself; she couldn't occupy herself with things that were common with others. No wonder she got the results she got; she was living her life differently than others.

Every man is consecrated to a plan – either God's or his own. We are to be consecrated to God's plan – that's the only way to fully accomplish it.

In Acts 26:19, Paul stood before King Agrippa and stated, *"...I was not disobedient unto the heavenly vision."* The heavenly vision God gave Paul for his life was what interested him – he was consecrated to that vision. That's how he was able to finish his race and fulfill the heavenly vision.

He wrote to Timothy,

2 TIMOTHY 4:6-8
6 For I am now ready to be offered, and the time of my departure is at hand.
7 I have fought a good fight, I HAVE FINISHED MY COURSE, I have kept the faith:
8 Henceforth there is laid up for me a crown of righteousness, which the Lord, the righteous judge, shall give me at that day: and not to me only, but unto all them also that love his appearing.

We are to run our race with our heavenly vision in mind. We are to run our race in line with what we are called to. That's what we are to be most interested in. That's what will bless our lives, our families, our local church, the Body of Christ, and the earth.

The Heavenly Vision for the Last Days

Kenneth E. Hagin announced by the Spirit the heavenly vision for this era of the last days. He said, "God is raising up strong local churches that move with the Word and the Spirit." I'm staying with the heavenly vision. I'm not going to veer into my own vision or into a different flow. I'm consecrated to that vision.

God doesn't dismiss and replace what He did previously, but He keeps building on it. God is doing what He's always done – only more of it.

The message God gave John the Baptist to preach is seen in Matthew 3:1 & 2, *"In those days came John the Baptist, preaching in the wilderness of Judaea, And saying, **Repent ye: for the kingdom of heaven is at hand.**"*

Then the next chapter of Matthew reads, *"Now when Jesus had heard that John was cast into prison, he departed into Galilee...From that time Jesus began to preach, and to say, **Repent: for the kingdom of heaven is at hand**"* (Matt. 4:12 & 17). Notice, when Jesus began to preach, He didn't preach a different message, but He picked up where John the Baptist left off and built on it.

A few chapters later, Matthew records what Jesus instructed when He sent His twelve disciples out to preach. *"And as ye go, preach, saying, **The kingdom of heaven is at hand.** Heal the sick, cleanse the lepers, raise the dead, cast out devils: freely ye have received, freely give"* (Matt. 10:7 & 8).

The book of Matthew shows the thread of the same message preached – from John the Baptist, to Jesus, who built on it, then to the twelve disciples, who carried it further.

That was the message for that era, and they carried that message further, building on it. They were not disobedient to the heavenly vision of their era – they were consecrated to it.

Vision of the Dry Riverbed

In the 1990s, my husband, who stood in the office of a prophet, had a vision regarding the era of the last days.

In the vision, he saw a boat full of people sitting in a dry riverbed. God told him that this boat represented a group of a previous era – they were stuck in a dry riverbed and didn't even know it. The people were singing, but it sounded terrible – they were off-key. They were toiling and sweating as they tried to row. They were working hard, but were going nowhere. They didn't even know there was no water in the riverbed. As they rowed the oars, dust was flying up from the sand and they were so excited – they thought it was the glory.

The pastor of these people stood up, and as he opened his mouth, a puff of dust came out – he didn't know he was dry; the people were deceived.

All of a sudden, my husband heard loud rejoicing, then he was picked up and taken to a place where there was a river flowing. In this river, he saw a group of people in a boat who weren't toiling or rowing; the flow of the river carried them. They were full of joy as they raised their hands, singing and praising God; their singing was beautiful.

The name of this group was on the side of the boat, "Whosoever Is Hungry and Thirsty." It didn't have any denominational name; it was going over those barriers.

Whoever was hungry and thirsty could get in this boat and in the flow of this river.

When the pastor of these people opened his mouth, the fire of God shot out.

My husband saw bottles floating in the water, and each of them had a note inside. One by one, he picked up bottles and read the notes. On each note was written a gift of the Spirit. All the nine gifts of the Spirit were in the flow of this river.

The people in the boat said, "This is wonderful. All our needs are met. Did you see that miracle? Did you see that one raised from the dead? Did you hear that word of knowledge? Did you see the gifts of the Spirit in operation? Did you see the gifts of healing, the working of miracles, the word of knowledge that prophet walked in?"

He said that the prophet's office will be revived as it was when they walked under that heavy anointing.

This is the Word and Spirit revival he saw. In this flow, all of our needs will be met. It won't be a struggle. It won't be by might, but by the river, which represents the flow of the Spirit and the anointing.

This vision shows what God is doing in this era, so that we will recognize His movement and be a part of it. God doesn't want any of us to be left out.

Just as we must be consecrated to God's will and plan for our lives so it can be fulfilled, we must also be consecrated to God's will and plan for this era so it can be fulfilled.

Promote the Message

It is also important that we be consecrated to His message. I'm not trying to promote and grow my ministry – I'm promoting God's message. That's what God is promoting – His message. When we stay with His message, we will be promoted.

It's not about our ministries, but it's about the message. As we stay with the message, we stay with the flow He is promoting, and we don't fall into the trap of trying to promote our ministries.

To be consecrated to the message means to separate from human plans and strategies to get ourselves and our ministries promoted. It means to separate from spiritual fads, messages of popularity, and winds of doctrine that have no enduring foundation. *"That we henceforth be no more children, tossed to and fro, and carried about with every wind of doctrine..."* (Eph. 4:14).

We want our lives and ministries to bear fruit, and promoting the message is what bears lasting fruit that brings glory to God.

Chapter 11

Great Discipline of the Spirit Over the Mind & Body

God said to me, *"To walk in this 'Double Portion' Anointing calls for great discipline of the spirit over the mind and body."*

To be successful in this, we must develop our spirits. The steps to developing our spirits are:

1. Meditate on the Word
2. Act on the Word
3. Give the Word first place
4. Instantly obey the voice of your spirit

#1 – Meditate on the Word

Joshua 1:8 instructs us, *"This Book of the Law shall not depart out of your mouth, but you shall meditate on it day and night, that you may observe and do according to all that is written in it. For then you shall make your way prosperous, and then you shall deal wisely and have good success"* (Amplified).

We develop our spirits as we meditate on the Word. We can't deal wisely in the affairs of life without meditating on the Word and doing it.

When we meditate on the Word, we are to look at every word and talk to God about it. Meditation is the Word and prayer working together – we are to talk to God about His Word.

Meditating on the Word involves muttering it and speaking it to ourselves so that we do it. Meditation on the Word enables us to deal wisely in the affairs of life and have good success as we make it a daily practice and lifestyle.

#2 – Act on the Word

James 1:22 instructs us, *"But be ye doers of the word, and not hearers only, deceiving your own selves."*

If we are a hearer only, and not a doer, we deceive ourselves. Christians become deceived by not being doers of the Word.

Being a doer of the Word means we are allowing the Word to govern us in our daily lives. No matter what arises in life, we are to ask ourselves, *What does the Word say about this?* And then act accordingly.

We must practice this daily. Those who were known for their spiritual lives kept practicing.

We are to primarily study the Epistles in the Word because they help us to know what to do.

#3 – Give the Word First Place

> **PROVERBS 4:20-22**
> **20 My son, attend to my words; incline thine ear unto my sayings.**
> **21 Let them not depart from thine eyes; keep them in the midst of thine heart.**
> **22 For they are life unto those that find them, and health to all their flesh.**

God and His Word are to be first in our lives. When faced with a situation, the first thing we should ask ourselves is, *What do God and His Word say about this?* Putting them last will lead us down a trail of tears, but putting them first will lead us down the path of life and health.

#4 – Instantly Obey the Voice of Your Spirit

Our spirit has a voice. Our spirit has no problem believing what God says because we have a brand new spirit. It's the unrenewed mind that has a problem with what God says.

In these last days, if we don't learn to follow our spirits, we will be deceived.

Practicing these four steps as part of our daily lifestyle will help develop our spirits, so our spirits can rule over and dominate our minds and flesh, keeping them in their rightful place.

If our minds or flesh rule and dominate us, they will lead us to failure and ruin, for they were not created to be in the lead. But when we're led by our spirits, we are led into success and victory.

A Strong Spirit

Proverbs 18:14 reads, *"The strong spirit of a man sustains him in bodily pain or trouble, but a weak and broken spirit who can raise up or bear?"* (Amplified).

Don't assume this is only referring to sickness and disease; it also refers to any trouble that comes.

What about when Paul and Silas were beaten and thrown in prison? (Acts 16). Their strong spirits sustained them, or dominated them, when they were in bodily pain and trouble. Because their spirits were strong, their spirits dominated them during that great trial instead of their minds; as a result, their faith flowed instead of fear, and victory came.

In 2 Corinthians 10:5, we are told, *"Casting down imaginations, and every high thing that exalteth itself against the knowledge of God, and bringing into captivity every thought to the obedience of Christ."*

This verse is a picture of a man's spirit exercising dominion over his mind. To walk in a great anointing, we must be highly developed and skillful in this.

There are those who don't pay attention to what they are allowing their mind to entertain – their minds are undisciplined and go unchecked, which makes for a troubled mind and a troubled life.

It is dangerous to leave the mind unguarded, for one wrong thought is an open door to the devil. Those who have strong spirits and those who walk in a great anointing cannot allow themselves a time when they are not bringing every thought into obedience to the Word.

We must also become skillful at turning toward our spirits instead of our minds. When we wake up in the middle of the night and first thing in the morning, we are to practice turning our attention and focus immediately toward our spirits, instead of toward our minds. Praising God is one of the best ways to do this. This must be practiced if we are to be skillful in it.

Those who carry a great anointing will face opposition, but if they are to remain peaceful, they can't practice turning toward their minds, but must be skilled at turning toward their spirits.

Paul and Silas were practiced at turning toward their spirits instead of their minds. After they were beaten and thrown in prison, they prayed and then sang praises unto God, which held them in the spirit realm (which is the faith realm), instead of getting into the mental arena.

After having been severely beaten, their minds could have entertained all kinds of thoughts like, *The ministry makes life hard. How could God permit this? I must be out of the will of God. I'm not appreciated. I'm getting out of the ministry.* No, they didn't entertain wrong thoughts because their spirits were strong and dominated their minds and bodies.

When tests and trials come, we can't afford to leave joy for one moment, for the joy of the Lord is our strength (Neh. 8:10), and if we get out of joy, we get out of strength.

The bodies of Paul and Silas were feeling the wrong thing that night, but because their spirits were stronger, they focused on and drew out of their spirits instead of their bodies. And when they did, they received a miracle that changed their situation.

Chapter 12

Great Accuracy

God told me in Russia, *"To walk in the 'Double Portion' Anointing calls for great accuracy."*

Walking in great accuracy includes walking in the Word, following the Spirit, and obeying the will of God for our lives.

To live accurately, we must possess accurate knowledge and understanding of the Word, we must walk in the light of the Word, follow the leading of the Spirit, and we must accurately understand and obey the will of God for our lives. Failure to do so can end up costing us much; it has even cost some their lives.

Follow the Word

It's dangerous to come up to light and not walk in it. When we see and understand what the Word shows or how the Spirit is leading us, we must walk in it, for when we walk in the light, we walk safely.

We can't walk accurately if we don't walk in wisdom. James 1:5 instructs us, *"If any of you lack wisdom, let him ask of God, that giveth to all men liberally, and upbraideth not; and it shall be given him."*

When we don't know how to handle a situation or how to get past opposition or a hurdle, we need to ask God for wisdom, believing that He will give it, and He will show us the exit out of the difficulty. Faith in the Word of God always works, but wisdom is knowing how to apply our faith properly in any given situation so that we get results.

Follow the Spirit

Proverbs 3:6 reads, *"In all thy ways acknowledge him, and* ***he shall direct thy paths****."* Proverbs 20:27 says, *"The spirit of man is the candle of the Lord...."* This simply means that the Lord will enlighten us or guide us through our spirits. When making decisions, we need to look to the Lord to direct us. How will He direct or guide us? Through our spirits.

When making a decision, if I don't sense any particular leading, then I follow the wisdom or the knowledge I have, because then what I know must be accurate for that situation. But if God leads me to do differently, then I lay down my own thinking and follow His direction.

I also look to the Lord to lead me in my leadership responsibilities – in overseeing the ministry, hiring staff, building or renovating, scheduling meetings, etc. I don't just move ahead without consulting with the Lord.

Changes in Fivefold Offices & in Direction in Ministry

To walk accurately, we must recognize if God is moving us into a different fivefold office or redirecting us in ministry. We must have the keenness to recognize His leadings so that we move with Him and stay in His will.

One of the things I so valued in my husband was how quick he was to recognize and move with God when He redirected him.

In 48 years of ministry, he pioneered three churches, pouring all his time, energy, and resources into them. But when God redirected him to move to different cities, he obeyed, turning two of those churches over to someone else. He didn't try to cling to them just because he had poured everything into them, and he didn't assume he would always be doing what he had been doing.

He also recognized that if he didn't move when redirected, everything would start drying up. Things don't dry up because God is withholding supply, but because the supply moves to where God tells us to be.

When things start drying up, some just think the devil is attacking; they don't recognize that God is redirecting them.

During a famine, God directed Elijah to dwell by the brook Cherith, and He supplied for him there. But after a time, the brook dried up and God redirected him; when he obeyed God and moved to the next place, he was fully supplied.

Just because our supply was once at a particular location doesn't mean it will always be there. The supply for our lives is where God tells us to be.

This is not only true about location changes, but also pertains to changes in a ministry office. We may stand in a fivefold office for a period of time, but if God moves us into another office, we must recognize that change. If we don't, things will start drying up.

It is dangerous to not move with God and to try to continue to occupy an office we are no longer anointed for.

If we don't move with God, we will be out of His will, which opens the door to the devil.

Through many years of ministry, we have seen churches dry up when pastors didn't make changes to be in the right locations, or they wouldn't move from the pastoral office into another office God had for them. We have also seen traveling ministries dry up when they were supposed to make a change to pastoring.

To be fully supplied, we must be where God tells us to be.

For 25 years I stood in the pastoral office. I loved being a pastor, but after 25 years God told me that I had come to the end of my pastorate. I didn't try to hold onto it. Faith moves with God – it doesn't try to stay where it's always been if God redirects.

I recognized that the anointing to pastor was no longer on me. If I would have tried to continue as pastor, the congregation would have suffered for it; they would not have had the pastoral anointing they needed, which would have been unsafe for them. And it would have been dangerous for me to try to occupy an office I was no longer anointed to stand in.

We must be keen to God's leadings, for our accuracy affects others as well as ourselves.

If things are drying up, get with God and find out why.

When things start drying up, some may say, "Well, God hasn't redirected me," so they assume they are on course and that the devil is just opposing them. But I have learned that God talks to us about what we talk to Him about. In other words, we have to initiate some conversations with Him. If things start drying up, ask God why. If we don't bring it up, He may not. "*...Ye have not, because he ask not*" (James 4:2).

Some don't have clarity because they don't ask.

What Are We To Emphasize?

When God redirected me out of the pastoral office into another office, He also redirected me in my teaching ministry.

As a pastor, I taught on many different topics because a pastor needs to address all the different aspects in the life of the sheep. When I left the pastoral office, I still continued to teach as I did when I was pastoring.

One day, God spoke to me and said, "You need to start feeding in line with the visions I've shown you." (I have had two visions and one dream where I saw the future of the ministry He has for me. One reason He showed me those was so I would prepare in those directions.) He told me, "You are still feeding yourself like a pastor, therefore you are still teaching like you're a pastor. You will teach in the direction you feed yourself on, so start feeding in line with the visions I've shown you, then you'll teach in that direction and you'll get into what you saw in those visions."

God not only moved me into a different office, but He redirected me in my teaching ministry, telling me what I was to emphasize. If I didn't make that change, I would have been out of the will of God.

Pastors need to teach on a wide variety of topics that apply to the lives of the sheep, but a traveling minister needs to know what they are to emphasize in their ministry. A pastor is like a doctor that is a general practitioner, but a traveling minister is like a specialist, who specializes in a particular direction.

For a minister to become rutted in any way can be dangerous to fulfilling God's plan and living accurately. We must be ready and willing to change if the Lord redirects us in any way.

I love something one pastor said. He had been a missionary for years when God called him to pastor. While pastoring, he said, "I always keep one bag packed in my closet. I want God to know I'm ready if He tells me to do something else."

We must live ready to make any changes so we can move with God.

God's Will Is My Home

Those who are not consecrated to God as they should be will struggle against how He's leading them.

For me, being consecrated includes not developing and holding to preferences. People sometimes struggle in obeying God's plan because they have developed a preference. When we develop a preference, then we give ourselves something to overcome if God directs us to do something other than our preference.

We still have our own wills, but I have made it my will to not have a preference, then I'm free to prefer what He prefers; I choose His will. This is part of being consecrated to the call and living accurately.

In my traveling ministry, I go where He directs me, which leads me all over the world. I have set my preference and will to be where He sends me. His will is my home. Wherever He sends me, that's my home. It is where I fit and belong.

When I arrive at a hotel in a foreign country or in the United States, I say, "Father, I'm thrilled to be here. It's my home, for Your will is my home." Then I am free to be there in complete joy and peace, not wishing I was somewhere else or impatient to leave; I'm free to give my all there, because it's my home.

When we think right and are consecrated to our calls, then the enemy can't draw us into any kind of dread, fear, depression, or complaining against what God leads us to do. His will is complete joy! This helps us to live accurately.

Don't Move Too Fast

To walk in accuracy, we must make sure we don't move too quickly and miss His leading. It's better to get behind in God's plan than get ahead of Him, for it's easier to catch up than to back up.

I endeavor to take time to get things clear in my spirit before making moves. If I have peace in my spirit about doing something, then I do it (even if my mind is being opposed). I just follow the peace in my spirit, for peace is the clarity. But if I don't have peace about it, then I don't do it.

We must learn to follow the Spirit and the peace that the Spirit gives if we are to live accurately.

Accuracy & Answers Every Day

Years ago, God said to me, "Start every day in the Spirit, then keep your heart turned toward Me all day long." This doesn't always mean having to take large segments of time in the morning, but it simply means to turn our attention and focus toward Him, which can be done by worshipping Him, praising and rejoicing, feeding on the Word, or praying. But the important thing is to do it from our spirits, not just our minds. Then we carry that mindfulness of Him throughout the day by keeping our hearts turned toward Him.

We are to bring this mindfulness of Him into our day. Young mothers can start their day in the Spirit by worshipping and rejoicing as they tend to their babies. Fathers can turn their attention toward Him as they ready themselves for the day. We can learn to turn our attention toward God in the tasks of our day.

In connection with that statement, God also dealt with me that I must take time to start every day in the Spirit, for my answers for that day are in the Spirit. As I start every day in the Spirit, I go further in the Spirit and gain the clarity I need for the decisions I must make throughout the day.

It's not hard to follow the Spirit, but we must take time to get in the Spirit so we can know how He's leading.

Luke 22:39 tells us, *"And He came out and went, **as was His habit**, to the Mount of Olives..."* (Amplified). Jesus' habit was to go to this grove of olive trees to pray. In His Father's presence He would see, hear, and know what to do regarding the things that would arise during the day.

As our ministries grow, we must make sure we hear and follow God accurately because so much is connected to making right decisions and right steps. We *must* take time to start every day in the Spirit, with our attention and focus on Him, then hold it there throughout the day.

Proper Order of Offices

For a minister who may stand in more than one office, it's important that the higher office is emphasized.

In the Word, the office of the apostle is listed first, the office of the prophet is listed second, and then the other three offices are listed after that.

If someone is an apostle or a prophet, those offices are higher than any of the other three offices they may stand in, so they must be emphasized above the others.

If they get their offices out of order, they will end up emphasizing a lower office instead of the higher office, which is out of line with the Word. If they do that, they will get out of the will of God.

In God's will, we are protected and kept safe, but being out of God's will opens the door to the devil.

Anyone with an anointing becomes a target of the devil because the anointing destroys his yokes. And as that anointing increases to a greater degree, even greater accuracy is called for, which helps safeguard us from the enemy.

Accuracy in fulfilling our calls will lengthen our lives, but being inaccurate can shorten them. That's one reason that God told me while in Russia that to walk in the "Double Portion" Anointing calls for great accuracy, for under a greater anointing, the margin for error is smaller.

Keeping multiple offices in their proper order, while not neglecting any of them, is part of walking accurately.

First Corinthians 14:4 reads, *"He that speaketh in an unknown tongue edifieth himself...."* One definition of the word "edify" is organize. So, we could read this verse as, "He that speaks in an unknown tongue organizes himself."

By speaking in tongues, we make ourselves more sensitive to the Holy Spirit, which helps us recognize how He's leading us. Knowing how He's leading us will help us to walk accurately in our ministry offices, while not neglecting any of them.

Understanding the Will of the Lord

God wants us to know and understand what His will is for our lives. Ephesians 5:17 instructs us, *"Wherefore be ye not unwise, but understanding what the will of the Lord is."* It's unwise to not understand what the will of the Lord is.

In light of this verse, one minister stated that every year he would lay out everything he was doing before the Lord to make sure he was on course and carrying out everything accurately. He would lay out before the Lord all that he was doing and how he was doing it and ask if he needed to do anything differently – if he needed to change something, add something, or leave off something.

It would benefit us all if we did the same thing, for it would assist us in walking accurately.

Someone may assume that if they needed to change anything that God would let them know. But as I stated previously, God talks to us about what we talk to Him about. Because He is a perfect gentleman, He will not always speak if He's not invited to; that's one reason we must ask Him.

There Must Be a Call To Stand in an Office

If operating inaccurately in the offices we're called to gives place to the devil, trying to operate in an office we're not called to would be dangerous.

To stand in a fivefold office requires a divine call and an anointing, so to try to function in an office without that call and the anointing would only mean failure.

No one can call someone else to the fivefold ministry – not family members, not a spouse, not a minister, and not even our own desire to do something for the Lord. God is the One who calls.

If someone is called to a fivefold ministry, they will have the witness of that in their spirit; God may even confirm it through a minister or someone else. But if someone doesn't have a witness in their spirit that they are called to a fivefold office, they are to just be faithful to serve God in their local church.

Every believer should serve in some role in their local church, and what a high honor that is! It is a different role than the fivefold ministry, but it is not a "less than" role.

Chapter 13

Pioneers of Faith – They Served Another

God told me in Russia, *"The pioneers of great faith walked in the 'Double Portion' Anointing.*

"The 'Double Portion' Anointing is available to those who are faithful to another man, as Elisha was to Elijah." (You can't just get in a ministry line and have hands laid on you to receive this.)

In saying this about faith pioneers, God was not only pointing to the anointing upon them, but also to how they came to walk in that degree of anointing.

The anointing upon a person's life can be increased by faithfulness, consecration, and diligence in the Word of God and prayer. But a "Double Portion" Anointing can only come when a man with the anointing exits the earth, and it can only come upon someone who was faithful to that man and followed him closely, just as it came upon Elisha at the exit of Elijah.

2 KINGS 2:8-14 *(Amplified)*
8 And Elijah took his mantle and rolled it up and struck the waters, and they divided this way and that, so that the two of them went over on dry ground.
9 And when they had gone over, Elijah said to Elisha, Ask what I shall do for you before I am taken from you. And Elisha said, I pray you, let a double portion of your spirit be upon me.
10 He said, You have asked a hard thing. However, if you see me when I am taken from you, it shall be so for you – but if not, it shall not be so.
11 As they still went on and talked, behold, a chariot of fire and horses of fire parted the two of them, and Elijah went up by a whirlwind into heaven.
12 And Elisha saw it and he cried, My father, my father! The chariot of Israel and its horsemen! And he saw him no more. And he took hold of his own clothes and tore them in two pieces.
13 He took up also the mantle of Elijah that fell from him and went back and stood by the bank of the Jordan.
14 And he took the mantle that fell from Elijah and struck the waters and said, Where is the Lord, the God of Elijah? And when he had struck the waters, they parted this way and that, and Elisha went over.

The *last* miracle we see done through Elijah is the parting of the Jordan, and the *first* miracle we see done through Elisha is the the parting of the Jordan. Under a double portion of the anointing, Elisha was able to pick up where Elijah left off and go on from there. All that Elijah accomplished enabled Elisha to start from where he had left off and go further. When Elisha took up that mantle, he didn't turn and go a different direction or course with that anointing, he continued in the same direction Elijah had been going; he did the same thing Elijah had just done.

In seeing Elisha do the same miracle as Elijah, we can't leave out the important truth that he was able to do that because he was faithful to closely follow Elijah throughout the many years he served him. While serving Elijah, he was not trying to go his own direction, do his own thing, or have his own ministry. He was doing everything he could to assist Elijah in what God had called him to do. In serving him faithfully, he gained knowledge and skill to walk in that anointing.

As we are faithful to closely follow a man that God brings to our lives and are good students of their example and instruction, we will advance alongside them and become skillful in that which they demonstrated and accomplished. Doing as they did, God can take us on further.

A double portion of the anointing enables a man to build on the previous and go further. However, if a man dishonors what was laid and accomplished by the previous generation or by the previous man he served, he disqualifies himself for that double portion of the anointing.

Esau failed to esteem, value, or honor his birthright and gave it away to Jacob, who did value and honor it.

We must recognize, value, and honor what God is doing if we are to participate in it.

They Served Another

God shows us that these faith pioneers were ones who walked with God, had robust faith, and produced much fruit because they closely followed another man. Joshua served Moses, Samuel served Eli, Elisha served Elijah, and Timothy served Paul. Before they were known as men of great faith, they were known to have faithfully served.

During previous seasons of their lives, their primary interest was not in having their own, but in serving another. They lost view of their own; their attention was on another. They loved the man, and they valued, prized, and honored what was in him. They used all their energies in helping another man succeed and fulfill his vision, and thereby received into their own lives the outcome of their faithfulness. In the service of another, they became students; they received the instruction, training, and divine impartations needed to fulfill their own call. They grew to have great faith as they took the path of faithfully serving another.

Jesus stated, *"And if ye have not been faithful in that which is another man's, who shall give you that which is your own?"* (Luke 16:12).

A man's zeal and ambition to have his own will not equip or qualify him for his own. Only wholehearted desire, honor, and service to see another man fulfill his call can position him to be trusted to have his own.

The leadership principles embraced by many portray that success is found only in having one's own. That is the mindset of the world, but it does not represent God and His way of promotion. Promotion from God comes through the avenue of honoring and serving another faithfully.

To serve under another while having one's own in view is unfaithfulness. It is a mistake to go through the *motions of serving*, while one's heart, motives, affections, and interests are set solely on themselves and getting their own. Yes, we can understand that the godly principle of serving another blesses our own life, but our motive is not to serve just so we can get our own. We don't just love what we can gain from a man, but we must love the man, otherwise we are not safe to serve him. We must lose sight of our own or we can't serve another wholeheartedly. As we lose sight of our own, only then can God safely promote us.

Many may go a lifetime serving another man, never having their own. If that is the will and plan of God for a man, what an honor! It takes a faithful man who loves and honors another to rightly succeed in that.

God is wanting us to see that before these faith pioneers of the past carried a great anointing, they were first wholehearted in serving another man.

That's a man God can promote.

The Path of Promotion

Consider Joseph and the path of his life. While growing up, he served his father as a shepherd. He was then sold into slavery where he served his master. Afterwards, he was wrongfully thrown into prison where he served under the prison keeper. He was then brought out of prison by Pharaoh and promoted to second-in-command in the nation. As a national leader, he served the Pharaoh and the people of the nation. Joseph's life was one of serving another man. However, his ultimate role was in serving God as he fulfilled His plan.

Two of Jesus' disciples sought leadership positions for themselves. The mother of James and John asked for Jesus to promote her sons to sit on His right and left hand in His Kingdom.

MATTHEW 20:25-28 *(Amplified)*
25 And Jesus called them to Him and said, You know that the rulers of the Gentiles lord it over them...
26 Not so shall it be among you; but whoever wishes to be great among you must be your servant,
27 And whoever desires to be first among you must be your slave –
28 Just as the Son of Man came not to be waited on but to serve, and to give His life as a ransom for many [the price paid to set them free].

The world sees success as a man having his own and ruling over others, but Heaven's definition of success is serving. At our highest, we serve – God and man.

This is living as Jesus lived – He served. He served through teaching, preaching, and healing, then ultimately in paying the price for the sin of all men.

Examples For Us

The faith pioneers of the past who walked under a "Double Portion" Anointing faithfully served another man of God. They were students of someone who knew God better than themselves, and they walked in what they were taught. They honored another. They didn't abandon those they were to serve; they stayed where God told them to be.

The faithfulness of these pioneers affected future generations; many enjoyed the fruits of their labor. Because of their obedience, they walked with God, received revelations of the Word, and produced much fruit, and through them God rewrote the stories of multitudes. That was accomplished through the "Double Portion" Anointing upon them, which they received by faithfully serving another.

It is of great importance for us to know what God did for them and through them, for they serve as examples of what God will do for us as we progress in this era of the Last Days. Their honor and faithfulness to serve turned them into examples that we can follow.

"Wherever you go, I will go..."

As a young man of 17, Lester Sumrall was raised up off his deathbed, then left home to conduct meetings in small country schoolhouses and churches. At the age of 19, he had a vision. He saw people from every nation running down the road of life, then at the end, falling off into hell – he saw the world going to hell. God was calling him to be a missionary to the world – he said yes.

A short time later, while conducting meetings in Oklahoma, God told him to go to Eureka Springs, Arkansas. It was there at a camp meeting that he met the English preacher Howard Carter. The young Sumrall walked up to meet the Englishman. He started to introduce himself, but to his surprise, the following words came out of his mouth instead. "Wherever you go, I will go. Over the highest mountains, over the tempestuous waves of the sea, into the deep valleys, into the plains. I will succor you, I will assist you. I will strengthen you, I will help you, and in every time of need I shall be with you. When you are old, I will succor you in your old age, and you shall be unto me as a father."

The young Sumrall was shocked at what he heard come out his mouth, but the English preacher wasn't. Three years earlier, while in prayer, God told him He was sending a young man to travel with him and assist him. He told him what the young man would say to him – the words the young Sumrall spoke.

For the next ten years, Lester Sumrall traveled around the world with Howard Carter, serving and assisting him in every way possible. He was receiving first-class spiritual training under this spiritual leader.

Dr. Sumrall became a general in the Body of Christ that God used to lead revivals that changed nations. The primary reason for that was because he first fully embraced the honor of loving and serving another man.

What You Honor, You Get to Participate In

In 2014, God spoke to me about another home. Although I already owned a home, He told me that He was going to give me the vacation home built by Aimee Semple McPherson, a well-known minister of the early 1900s. In 2015, I was able to purchase the wonderful, historical home that had been completed in 1929.

After purchasing it, I often told God how much I appreciated Him giving it to me. I thought about how there had possibly been many others who would have liked to have owned the home, but God had me in mind for it. How it blessed me to know that God thought of me for the home.

As I was rehearsing this to God, He spoke to me. "What you honor, you get to participate in." The regard and honor I held for the faith pioneers became an avenue that God could bless me through. Honor brought me increase.

This a great truth of how God operates – what you honor, you get to participate in. When you honor what God is doing through another man, you can receive of what is upon them and what they walk in.

That would also be true regarding the Word. The portion of the Word you honor is the portion of the Word you get to participate in. If you honor the Word regarding healing, you get to participate in healing. If you honor the Word regarding prosperity, you get to participate in prosperity. However, the flip side of that would be true as well – what you fail to honor, you can't participate in – you dismiss yourself from it.

Mark 6 tells of when Jesus was in His own hometown.

MARK 6:3-6
3 ...And they were offended at him.
4 But Jesus, said unto them, A prophet is not without HONOUR, but in his own country, and among his own kin, and in his own house.
5 And he could there do no mighty work, save that he laid his hands upon a few sick folk, and healed them.
6 And he marvelled because of their unbelief....

Because they didn't honor Him, they couldn't receive from Him.

It takes honor to receive from God. It takes honor to recognize and to receive of what is honorable. It takes honor to recognize God in another man and faithfully serve him.

Faith pioneers walked in great honor, or they never would have been able to move with God as they did, walking in the degree of anointing they walked in.

If we are to walk in the "Double Portion" Anointing, we can't expect to walk any differently. Honor is such a languishing quality in today's society, but it is mandatory if one is to walk with God and under a greater or a "Double Portion" Anointing.

When we live a life of honor, when we honor men of God He connects us to and we honor what God has done in the past, we position ourselves for God to repeat that through us.

I want to see what they saw, but in an even greater way.

Chapter 14

Skill With the Anointing & Call

In Russia, God said to me, *"Walking in a 'Double Portion' Anointing calls for great skill with the anointing and with the call that's entrusted to you."*

We must have an accurate understanding of what we are called to if we are to become skillful with that call and the anointing. As we spend time in the Word and in prayer, including praying in other tongues, we can know what we are called to; God will reveal it to us.

Many make the mistake of deciding what they want to do, then labeling that as what God is calling them to. I have heard pastors tell how they thought they were called to the traveling ministry and traveling ministers who thought they were called to pastor. They later realized that what God was calling them to was different than what they had thought.

We need to know our job description in the Body of Christ. We need to know the office we are called to, then be faithful to stay in it. It's dangerous to try to walk in an office we're not called to.

Discern Your Part

My husband discussed with another leading minister something they had observed in their many decades of ministry. They estimated that 50% of churches were being pastored by men who weren't called to pastor. Instead, these men should have been helping another pastor. They weren't accurately discerning their part in the Body of Christ.

Many sense a compelling to do something for God, then mislabel it as a call to pastor or to have their own traveling ministry. A desire to do something for God is not a call to a fivefold office; all of God's people should have that desire.

With that compelling to do something for God, first they should make sure they're plugged in and staying put in a local church, helping their pastor fulfill the vision God gave him without entertaining any desire or motive of having their own. Then, if God has something more for them, He will let them know. If God doesn't call them to the fivefold ministry, then they'll already be in the right place by helping another pastor.

Many want their own because they don't see or haven't been taught the great honor of serving another man. The Holy Spirit is called the Helper. It is a position worthy of the Godhead. One member of the Trinity is a Helper. Being a helper is not beneath any of God's children – it is a position of great honor. It is not a "less than" role. It takes a renewed mind to see the great honor of serving another man and his vision.

Know Your Job Description in the Body of Christ

We will struggle in life and in ministry if we don't agree with the call of God on our lives, don't stay in our office, or complain against our call. But if we will agree with God and stay in the office we are called to, we will be the happiest, have the most success, and bear the most fruit.

Every believer, even if they aren't called to a fivefold office, needs to know their job description in the Body of Christ and their role in their local church. As my husband said, "If you don't know your place in the Body of Christ, then start serving in your local church where your natural abilities are, then your supernatural abilities will start kicking in."

Jesus knew what He was called to and was skillful with the anointing. In the book of Luke, Jesus gave the job description of the anointing upon Him.

> **LUKE 4:18 & 19**
> **18 The Spirit of the Lord is upon me because He has anointed me to preach the gospel to the poor; he hath sent me to heal the brokenhearted, to preach deliverance to the captives, and recovering of sight to the blind, to set at liberty them that are bruised,**
> **19 To preach the acceptable year of the Lord.**

Acts 2:22 reads, "*...Jesus of Nazareth, a man approved of God among you by miracles and wonders and signs, which GOD DID BY HIM....*" God is the One who did the miracles through Jesus, but Jesus was skillful in allowing God to flow through Him unhindered.

No one who came to Jesus in faith for healing failed to receive their help, because Jesus never hindered power from flowing through Him. He was skillful at being the channel that God could flow through.

If we hinder the flow, then we limit what God can do through us. We are to become skillful at allowing God to flow through us unhindered.

A Vision of Jesus

In the early 1990s, my husband had a vision during one of his services. (I tell this vision because although it happened to him, it benefits us.) In the vision, Jesus appeared to him, and fire shot out of His eyes as He said, "You're not being skillful with the healing anointing!" Then He disappeared.

(In 1971, Jesus put a healing anointing in my husband's right hand, and multitudes have been healed as a result.)

Jesus was displeased that Ed was not being skillful. Fire shooting out of Jesus' eyes shows us how important skill is to Him, because if we aren't skillful, we hinder God from operating and moving through us the way He wants to.

Specifically speaking, Jesus talked to my husband about being skillful with the healing anointing, which wouldn't apply to everyone. But generally speaking, He was talking about being skillful, which would apply to everyone. We are to become skillful with our calls, anointings, giftings, endowments, and anything entrusted to us.

Some make the mistake of just relying on a call, a talent, or their love for the Lord to put them over. But those are no substitute for being skillful.

God can only manifest His power through us to the level of our skill. The greater our skill, the greater the degree of power that can flow.

Whatever you're called to, study and get around those who are skillful in "like" calls. Get around those who know God better than you, then be a good student.

If there is a profession or business endeavor God leads you into, study, learn, and become skillful in it. Be a student of someone who is skillful in that field.

As believers, we are all to become skillful – skillful with the Word and walking in love, skillful with our faith, joy, peace, and all of the other nine fruits of the spirit, skillful with healing power, skillful in prayer, skillful in giving and receiving, in serving, in ministering to others, in walking in the Spirit, skillful at guarding our thought lives, and skillful with anything else connected to living a victorious life and in being a blessing to others.

It is our responsibility to see to it that we become skillful – not God's.

Good & Faithful

Matthew 25:21 refers to those who had been faithful with the talents given them. *"His lord said unto him, Well done, thou* ***good*** *and* ***faithful*** *servant: thou hast been faithful over a few things, I will make thee ruler over many things: ENTER THOU INTO the joy of thy lord."*

Notice the two things that pleased their lord about the servants – they were good, and they were faithful. If we're to be successful, we must be "good" or skillful at our jobs. If we don't become "good" or skillful with our jobs, then we're not being "faithful." Success requires skill.

In the business world, to please your boss, you must know your job and be skillful at carrying it out. To be promoted in your field, you must be skillful.

The Amplified translation reads, *"...I will put you in charge of MUCH. ENTER INTO and share the joy (the delight, the blessedness) which your master enjoys."* The servants that were good and faithful with what was entrusted to them were promoted into more.

The reward of skill and faithfulness is "more." For the believer, that would mean more revelation, more anointing, more increase – more! Progress and promotion come as we grow in skill and faithfulness.

Be a Good Student

To be skillful with our call and the anointing upon our lives, we must be trained. We must recognize those God brings into our lives to help train us and be faithful to follow and stay with them. We must never enter into the risky path of being "self-taught."

My husband made the statement, "When someone has a call and an anointing on their life, God will lead them to the right people to help train them in their call and in that anointing." But they have to remain faithful to that man to be trained. Someone may have an anointing on their life, but they'll never be able to walk in the full measure of that anointing unless they are trained.

My husband also said, "When God gives someone an anointing, He expects them to get around the right men to help develop that anointing. If they don't develop that anointing, then they are out of the will of God." And it's when we are out of the will of God that we open the door to the devil.

Having a call places a responsibility on us to be faithful to be taught and trained.

Now, that training process can look differently for different people. Some will be trained as Elisha was with Elijah, traveling and working closely with him every day. Jesus taught and trained His disciples as they lived and traveled with Him. Others have the opportunity to be taught and trained as they serve in a volunteer position around a man of God, while others may be on a man's staff.

Every believer needs to be taught and trained. Although they may not be called to stand in a fivefold office, they still have a place to fulfill and a supply to bring to the Body of Christ, primarily through serving in their local church. Their pastor is the one who is to teach and train them in fulfilling the will of God for their lives, along with the help of other fivefold offices their pastor may bring into the church.

Fivefold Offices Are To Assist & Aid the Pastoral Office

Actually, all the fivefold offices are to be an assist and an aid to the pastoral office. The pastoral office is not the most powerful office, but it is the most important office, for it is the pastor that oversees the daily welfare of the sheep.

No one can live a successful Christian life without having a pastor. Matthew 9:36 shows this. *"But when he saw the multitudes, he was moved with compassion on them, because they fainted, and were scattered abroad, as sheep having no shepherd."*

It doesn't say they fainted and were scattered because they didn't have an apostle, or a prophet, or an evangelist, or a teacher – but because they didn't a shepherd, a pastor. The pastoral office carries an anointing to help keep the people from fainting in their race and from being scattered in their lives.

Everyone who stands in a fivefold office should have a proper understanding of this and show proper regard and honor toward the pastoral office, pointing the people toward the pastoral office.

The apostle, prophet, evangelist, and teacher are to add to and build up the local church, pointing any new converts toward having a pastor and being plugged into a local church.

Charles Finney had some of the most enduring fruit through the revivals he conducted. He not only had a great number of converts that were born again, but the highest percentage of those converts continued on in their spiritual life by becoming part of a local church. Actually, Finney would only count as fruit those who became part of a local church.

Even though the fivefold offices are to assist and aid the pastor in building the local church, that does not include telling a pastor how to run his church. The pastor will have the anointing, the vision, and the wisdom to oversee his church, not the other traveling ministries.

Everyone who stands in a fivefold office must have a pastor for their own life and for their family. Even though a man may have a traveling ministry and not be home to attend services in his local church, his family needs to be under the anointing of the pastor, and he needs that anointing in his life. Without this, his life and family will suffer greatly.

Stay Put

Just as sheep must stay with their shepherd so they can be taught and trained, those called to stand in an office or ministry must stay with the ones God brings into their lives if they are to receive what they need to fulfill their calls.

Being with a man of God does not ensure our success. Judas was a bad student and didn't fulfill what he was called to, even though Jesus personally taught and trained him. It is our hunger and the condition of our hearts that determine how good of a student we are.

Having a call to stand in a fivefold office does not ensure our success; we must be good, faithful students.

If we are to receive all we should as students of another man, we must be consecrated to that season. We must not waste our opportunity and become distracted, giving ourselves to other things that rob our time and attention from our training and preparation; we must take advantage of every opportunity to serve and receive from them.

One must be wholehearted in the training and preparation seasons of their life, giving their all to them, for those seasons are never lost or wasted time. Those seasons are to be valued, honored, and embraced if we are to be skillful in what we are called to. The more diligent and faithful we are to our preparation, the more progress we will make.

It is not God's plan for any of us to bypass training and preparation. We must stay where God puts us, not jumping from one man to another, and not jumping from one pastor to another; our faithfulness to those God brings into our lives will *accelerate* us in our spiritual development.

Dr. Ed Dufresne – Faithful To Follow

As a new convert in his mid 20s, my husband served in many capacities in his local church. As God prepared him further for his call, He spoke to him to attend a particular convention. When Ed told God he didn't have the money to attend, He told him to sell his house, and he did. It sold the next day.

Ed attended the conference and was introduced for the first time to the ministries of Pastor John Osteen, Kenneth Copeland, and Kenneth E. Hagin. The ministries of these men played key roles in training Ed for what he was called to. Through the years, the anointing on them nourished the call and mantle upon his life in different ways.

During the conference, Ed purchased their tapes and books, and then for months he locked himself up in his garage with them. It was after that season that doors of ministry began to open to him.

His training didn't end there. God spoke to Ed that if he was going to walk in what He had for him, Kenneth E. Hagin was to be his spiritual father, and he was to follow him closely. No, that didn't mean for Ed to seek personal attention from Brother Hagin, trying to know him after the flesh, but he was to take every opportunity to be in his services to be trained and to have his own mantle nourished.

For the next 30 years, he was faithful to obey God in that. We had many opportunities to be in services and in more personal settings with Brother Hagin. What God did for us through this man and his ministry rewrote the story of our lives.

Ed sold his house to be where God told him to be, and because of it, God was able to bring him into the next thing he had for him. It set him on course for his ministry and future. No, God won't tell every man to sell his house, but every man must obey God if he is to get into all that God has for him.

It was a few years after that when God brought Dr. Lester Sumrall into Ed's life. My husband was in his services, fed on his materials, and was given the opportunity to travel with him and preach alongside him. Because Ed honored him and obeyed God to follow him, God used Dr. Sumrall to greatly impact and affect my husband's life and ministry.

My husband was faithful to honor and follow the men God put in his life, and for almost 30 of those years, I was alongside him in this great privilege. We didn't get distracted by others, but stayed with the men God connected us to. As a result, the mantles on our lives were nourished.

For those with a call, there is one primary person God will put in their life to follow closely. However, especially if someone is called to more than one ministry office, God may also use others to teach them, just like He did with my husband.

In 1 Corinthians 4:14-16 Paul writes, "*...as my beloved* ***sons*** *I warn you. For though ye have ten thousand instructors in Christ, yet have ye not many* ***fathers****: for in Christ Jesus I have* ***begotten you through the gospel.*** *Wherefore I beseech you,* ***be ye followers of me.***"

Paul calls them his "sons," thereby calling himself their father, and he tells them to follow him. Since he was a father to them, he was beseeching them to follow him. By following him, they could stay on the course God had for them and not be distracted by another.

"I Long To See You That I May Impart Unto You..."

Someone may already be in the full-time ministry, but that doesn't mean they don't need someone to speak into their lives. Our blessing is connected to another man, and we need to know who that is and stay connected to them. In doing so, we can receive the impartations we need to fulfill what we are called to.

In Romans 1:11, Paul writes, *"For I long to see you, that I may impart unto you some spiritual gift, to the end ye may be established."* The Amplified translation reads, *"For I am yearning to see you, that I may impart and share with you some spiritual gift to strengthen and establish you."*

Paul was writing to them, teaching them the revelations God had given him, but he acknowledged that that was not enough. To impart that which would establish and strengthen them further, he needed to see them. Without receiving the proper impartations, they would be lacking.

No one can receive all God has for them through a man by way of a letter, a book, a recording, or a computer screen. At some point, the man of God needs to see them in person so that impartations can come.

Don't misunderstand me, we can receive much through these other avenues, but none of them are meant to take the place of being present where the man of God is; then impartations can be received in a particular way.

In John Wesley's commentary on the Bible, he states regarding this verse that the impartations can come by the laying on of hands, prayer, preaching the Gospel, and private conversations.

Not everyone has the opportunity to be with men of God in private settings, but impartations can still be received by sitting under their preaching and teaching. Taking advantage of the opportunities to be in their services will make impartations into your life that will establish and strengthen you.

Through the many years of having personal conversations and being in private settings with men of God, we have received answers and help for our lives in a very particular way. These conversations served to safeguard and accelerate us in our lives and ministry.

It is possible to get behind spiritually and in ministry. When ministers and believers are not in the services of those they are to follow, they don't receive all God has for them, and they fall behind. Without needed impartations, they won't be able to advance to the next level and to all the phases of their ministry as they should. However, if they get behind, they can also catch up if they will correct themselves.

Some ministers fail to get in services with their spiritual fathers because they are trying to save money or they are spending their time on other things. They are only robbing from their calls and spiritual progress.

My Bible School

Dad Hagin was a spiritual father to my husband and me, and Dr. Sumrall was our pastor. However, when they both went to Heaven, my husband filled those roles in my life. All along, my husband had been my Bible school, and I had a particular privilege few get of living with their Bible school. Since he was 20 years older than me, he had already been in the ministry almost 20 years when we married, so I had a lot of catching up to do.

When he was in the pulpit, he was no longer just my husband, but more than that, he was a prophet of God with answers for my life, so I received him as such.

When married to a minister, if someone doesn't recognize their spouse for the office they stand in and doesn't receive from them as they should, their life will suffer for it. They won't receive the answers they need, and it could cost them much, even their lives in some cases.

I recognized and received my husband as the man of God he was, and my life was blessed for it.

Years ago, God spoke to me, "You do everything you can to see to it that your husband fulfills his call, and I will see to it that you fulfill yours." He was assuring me of His divine help as I sowed my help toward my husband.

God was instructing me that even though I was called to the fivefold ministry, I was first to be the appropriate helpmeet to my husband and to his call. I was not looking to have my own ministry apart from his; I was an assist to him. In assisting him, my ministry would be fulfilled. We must sow if we are to reap.

Once my husband moved to Heaven, I immediately looked to the Lord as to who I was to follow and who was to speak into my life. God used one particular man to minister to me by the Spirit; I paid attention to who God used to speak to me. God dealt with me that I was to follow this man. Being accountable to someone who speaks into my life and ministry blesses my life and is a safety for me, my family, and my ministry.

I am not only to receive a supply through him, but I am also to bring a supply to him through prayer, being in his meetings, and giving financial support.

When God shows us who to follow, it's not just so we can *receive* a supply through them, but also so we can *bring* a supply to them through prayer, meeting attendance, financial giving, and any other way we can. What an honor to have a divine connection in our lives! Nothing else can substitute for them.

Safe To Follow

In studying faith pioneers of the past, we are not to follow those too closely who didn't finish right, or the same thing could happen to us. There are some who had a strong, bold faith, and as a result, God worked great miracles, but they got off in their doctrine. We can follow their faith, but not their doctrine.

In other words, don't just swallow everything. Just because someone flourished in one aspect of their call and ministry doesn't mean they were accurate in every aspect. We need to recognize that.

Chapter 15

A Smaller Margin for Error

God said to me in Russia, *"The greater the anointing, the smaller the margin for error."*

This is also a statement God had made to me many years ago. My husband and I had preached for a precious pastor who died suddenly in his mid 50s. I had asked God about that, not because it made me waver in my faith, but because I wanted to learn as much as I could through the situations of others. God answered me, "The greater the anointing, the smaller the margin for error." I knew that there was error on that pastor's side somewhere that opened the door to his premature death.

The phrase, "The greater the anointing, the smaller the margin for error," is in keeping with the verse found in Luke 12:48, "*...For unto whomsoever much is given, of him shall be much required: and to whom men have committed much, of him they will ask the more.*"

The devil hates the anointing. He will work for years and decades to bring someone into bondage to something. Then when they come into contact with the anointing for one moment, that bondage is utterly destroyed. Years of the devil's work is destroyed in a moment – no wonder he hates it.

That anointing can come through the teaching or preaching of the Word, through a gift of the Spirit, through the laying on of hands, or through speaking the Word. Therefore, the anointing upon someone makes them a target for the enemy.

As we stay in God's will and plan for our lives, we are protected and kept safe. But if we get out of our calls, disobey God, or fail or omit to do something He instructed, then we open the door to the devil.

Wisdom

In studying faith pioneers of the past, I noticed that most of those who had great success earlier on in their lives and ministries died prematurely. Because it takes time to learn, grow, and develop in wisdom, it seems that being younger when success came, they didn't have the time necessary to gain the wisdom needed to walk in a greater anointing. Longevity is to be our goal, not early success.

We must not only gain knowledge and skill in our calls and anointings, but we must also gain the wisdom needed to fulfill our calls and to walk under a greater degree of the anointing. Being called, being anointed, and even having strong faith is never meant to take the place of wisdom. It requires wisdom to run our race and finish accurately; that's why we must prize wisdom.

We have something to do with determining the degree of the anointing we walk in. We can increase the anointing upon our lives by faithfulness, consecration, and diligence in the Word of God and prayer. But as we increase in the anointing, we must make certain we are also growing in wisdom, for it helps safeguard us.

The anointing is the greatest power in existence, so we must have the wisdom to carry it and operate in it; lack of wisdom opens the door to the devil.

Obedience

My husband would also warn young ministers by giving his testimony of a test he faced. My husband was very high energy. In his own words, "I didn't have any quittin' sense!" That may be okay when you're younger, but as you get older, you have to use wisdom in pacing yourself.

God would deal with my husband about resting more, and for a short time he would, then he'd slip back into his old ways.

When he reached his mid 50s, Ed was diagnosed with cancer. The day he was diagnosed, he asked God, "Okay God, I know You don't miss it. I've missed it somewhere. Where did I miss it and open the door to the devil?"

Immediately God answered him. "Two things. First, you didn't rest your body like I told you to. Second, you haven't been obeying Me in the prophet's office. I would tell you to say certain things and you wouldn't because of what people might say."

Ed repented, then God said, "Alright, it will all be gone within 30 days." He did have some measure of treatment, but when he went back to the doctor on day 28, the doctor said, "It's all gone. Someone up there likes you!"

Things we used to get by with, we can no longer get by with as the anointing upon us increases. We must be obedient to God in all things so that we keep the door closed to the enemy.

I Magnify My Office

One way we can get into error is by not thinking right about our call and the office we stand in.

Some are fearful, have a bad self image, are insecure, or don't like being in front of people. Because of that, they complain against their call and draw back from it. When they don't obey God in their call, others are robbed from – they don't receive what they need. In drawing back, they get out of the will of God, and then the devil can attack them.

They must renew their minds further; they must deal with that wrong thinking and quit letting those thoughts steal from them. They must consecrate themselves to the call of God; that's the place of safety.

The enemy will use all different kinds of strategies to try to get us to think wrong about the office we stand in or about things connected with that office, for when we think wrong, we will struggle.

Another thing we must guard against is boredom. Some become bored with the office they stand in and wander into another man's office; that is unsafe. Entertaining wrong thoughts of boredom can lead us off course.

We must also guard against disappointments that may come. We may be tempted to become disappointed with people or situations, but we must not blame the ministry or the call of God for any disappointments caused by other people.

We must think right toward the office we are called to so that we honor it as we should and not be tempted to do something else when faced with opposition.

Paul stated, *"...I magnify mine office"* (Rom. 11:13). It is an honor to be called to a fivefold office; it must be treated with honor and regard. Paul highly esteemed the office he stood in – he magnified it. He didn't diminish it with wrong thoughts or wrong attitudes.

How we approach and treat our office will set the tone for how others treat it. Others must have proper regard for the office we stand in if they are to receive from it.

We must guard our thoughts against complaint. To complain against what we are called to or the things connected to our office, is to complain against the will of God, and that's dangerous.

Someone may entertain wrong thoughts of how their life was easier or how much more money they were making before they entered the ministry. Being in the will of God blesses our lives, but thinking wrong toward our call and the will of God makes life hard. It's wrong thinking that makes life hard, not the will of God.

Hebrews 11:15 tells us, *"And truly, if they had been mindful of that country from whence they came out, they might have had opportunity to have returned."*

If someone holds more regard for a previous season than for what God is bringing them into, they will be tempted to return to things of the past. They are not consecrated as they should be and don't hold proper regard for what they are called to, and until they correct themselves, they will continue to struggle.

Nothing we have done in the past equals the honor of what God is bringing us into.

We must guard our thought lives so we think right toward our call, toward things connected to our call, and toward His will for our lives.

As the anointing increases on our lives, so must our honor toward our call and God's plan. We are to follow Paul's example in saying, "I magnify my office."

Chapter 16

Right Fellowship & Divine Connections

While in Russia, God said to me, *"Walking in a 'Double Portion' Anointing demands right fellowship and protecting right connections to divine supplies in your life."*

I cannot overemphasize the importance and blessing that are connected to having right fellowship. It refreshes us in our race like nothing else can. The fellowship of those God has brought into my life is one of the things I value, love, and honor most in life; I treat it with great regard.

Paul stated, *"I am glad of the coming of Stephanas and Fortunatus and Achaicus: for that which was lacking on your part they have supplied. For they have refreshed my spirit and yours: therefore acknowledge ye them that are such"* (1 Cor. 16:17 & 18).

The Amplified translation of verse 18 reads, *"For they gave me respite from labor and rested me and* ***refreshed my spirit*** *as well as yours.* ***Deeply appreciate and thoroughly know and fully recognize such men."***

Notice the wording used, "...Deeply appreciate and thoroughly know and fully recognize...." We need to know and recognize those God gives to our lives so that we appreciate them as we ought, giving them a place in our lives.

Notice what these men did for Paul – they refreshed his spirit. The fellowship God brings to our lives will refresh us in a way that nothing else or no one else does. I believe that many don't recognize the value of refreshing that comes this way.

Being around fellow believers is to refresh us, but Paul singled out that there were certain men who brought a refreshing to him. There are certain people that refresh us in a particular way. Know who those people are – recognize and value them and what they bring to your life.

When a marathon runner is in a race, all along the route are refreshment tables. As they run by, they grab something off the table that refreshes them in their race – it helps them keep running. Coaches and trainers will also come up alongside them and shout out encouragements, instructions, and reminders of their training so that they finish as they should.

That's what these precious men and women of God do for our lives. They refresh us in our race so that we are encouraged to keep running as we ought, especially when we are faced with tests and challenges. They will give us encouragement and remind us of what we have been trained in. They bring a precious and much-needed supply to us in the race we are running.

Through my years of ministry, I have seen the benefit this refreshing brings, but I have also seen the condition of those ministers who have not put themselves around right fellowship so that they could be refreshed. Paul stated that these men gave him respite from labor, rested him, and refreshed his spirit. Those who don't take advantage of the opportunity to be around right fellowship don't receive the respite, rest, and refreshing they could receive. As a result, they grow weary as they labor alone.

In this rich fellowship that belongs to us, we are not only to receive refreshing, but we are to be mindful to bring a refreshing to others. We may never fully realize how our fellowship will impact someone else in their race.

Right fellowship refreshes us, but it also encourages us to stay on course in our race, not veering off; it encourages us to run accurately. Right fellowship won't distract and draw us into a direction where we don't belong. Therefore, we must recognize who those are that encourage us in the right direction. We are to *"...deeply appreciate and thoroughly know and fully recognize such men."*

God told me in Russia that to walk in a double portion of the anointing, it *demands* right fellowship.

Our Own Company

It's important that we run our race with those that God has put into our lives and not veer off on our own or look for someone different to join ourselves to. We must run with those who are running the same direction – those who are in the same flow God has for us.

The words of those around you will get in your ears. They can either encourage and fortify you in your race, or they can take you off course. Who we are running with affects us in our race.

When we run with those of our own company, it makes a difference for us.

Peter and John ministered to the lame man at the Gate Beautiful, and he was healed. They were then brought before the chief priests and elders who threatened them. When they were released, Acts 4:23 tells us what they did, *"And being let go, **they went to their own company,** and reported all...."* At a time of opposition, they didn't go just anywhere – they went back to those of their own company. They knew who their company was.

It's important that we know who our company is, for then we know where to go in times of opposition. We will find our greatest refreshing with those who are in our own company.

That doesn't mean that we are divisive and exclude ourselves from the rest of the Body of Christ and other Christians. We love, value, and appreciate the whole Body of Christ, but we need to know where we fit. By staying in our company and where we fit, we are adding to the health and well-being of the Body of Christ. It causes problems for us and the Body if we are out of place, being where we don't fit.

Where do we fit? Where God tells us to be. We don't fit just anywhere; there is a specific place where we fit.

In the body, the hand doesn't fit just anywhere. The hand has to be joined to the wrist, or it won't be able to function right. The hand can't decide to be joined to the shoulder or to the knee or to the foot – it can't function there. Yes, the hand is part of the body, but it has to be in the right place if it's to function right.

Even so, we must be where God instructs us to be because that is where we fit and where we will function as we ought.

To walk in a greater anointing, we must know where our company is and stay with that company. To leave our company is to leave where we fit, and then we won't be able to function in the Body of Christ as we ought.

Being Rightly Connected

We can know where our company is and where we fit, but we also have to protect that connection.

In building a car engine, it's not enough to just stack up all the parts under the hood – they have to be in the right place. Even when a part is in place, it has to be rightly connected. If the connection is loose, the engine won't work right.

Likewise, we have to be in the right place – where we fit. Even then it's not enough to just know where we fit; we have to be rightly connected. We must have a strong, tight connection – not a loose one – or we won't function right.

Appreciating another man's ministry by reading his materials and listening to his recordings does not define being rightly connected. At some point, you have to be present where he is, in his services.

Ministers and believers alike have to be rightly connected; a loose connection will mean difficulty.

If a believer is a part of the right church, but seldom attends, they are loosely connected, and things in their life aren't going to function right. Being loosely connected, they won't bring the supply they should, and they won't receive the supply they need.

Likewise, a minister may know who they are to be connected to, but if they seldom put forth the effort to be in the services of that person, they are loosely connected. Without a right connection, they are not going to bring the supply they should or receive the supply they should.

Pastors can become disappointed when congregation members are unfaithful and inconsistent toward their local church, but we need to make sure we are doing the same thing we expect out of our congregation members – being faithful and consistent to be where we should be. We are not to attend services as little as possible, but as much as possible.

Guest Ministers of the Same Company

In pastoring, I stayed with my own company. By that, I mean that I brought in guest ministers to preach in the church who were of my company. Don't misunderstand me. I value and honor all those that stand in fivefold offices, but by staying in my own company, the guest ministers I brought in fed the congregation the same diet I was feeding them; therefore, the sheep weren't confused by what was ministered.

The following illustration shows what I mean. When I travel to foreign countries, I try to eat the foods that are most like what my system is used to. Some countries have very different items cooked with different spices. It doesn't mean it's not good food – it's just not served up in a way that my system is used to, so I stay away from some of those things.

Likewise, by having guest ministers that are in my company, they serve up the Word in a way that the congregation is used to, so it doesn't confuse or unsettle them. That protects the flow that God has us in. Therefore, when guest ministers do come, we have a flow in our church that accommodates them and allows them to function in their office at a higher degree.

In a neighborhood, there are many homes. But I don't go to just any home to eat, I go to mine; that's where the dinner table that feeds me is located. Spiritually, I don't eat off many different tables. I know the table that feeds me. In pastoring, I brought that same understanding to our church. I don't feed the sheep off many tables, but one table – the table of my company. That's why our church is healthy.

When staying with the ministers in my company, there is a fit and a flow in the services that blesses everyone – the minister and the congregation. There is a divine connection, and everyone recognizes that it's something God puts together, and that's what produces the greatest fruit.

Divine Supplies

Those of our own company are divine supplies, but a spiritual father or spiritual parents are also a divine supply in our lives.

Paul instructed, *"Be ye followers of me, even as I also am of Christ"* (1 Cor. 11:1). Our success is connected to another man. The more closely we follow them, the better we'll finish.

Divine supplies help in our spiritual progress. One way to progress in our walk with God is to be around someone who knows God better than us. My husband used to say, "Get around someone who knows God better than you, then shut up!" Don't do all the talking – listen!

When called to a fivefold office, God will put someone in your life to follow closely. Following him rightly and wholeheartedly helps train and hold you to the course God has for you.

If someone doesn't know who that person is in their life, they are not in position to reach the highest flow for their life and ministry.

One pastor told of being raised an orphan, and because he didn't have parents, there were many difficulties he faced that could have been avoided if he would have had parents to help train and guide him. He longed to have parents.

When we closely follow the spiritual parents God gives us, there are so many traps, difficulties, and hardships that we avoid.

Nothing else can take the place of having those divine supplies in our lives.

Who is your spiritual father or your spiritual parents? Who is your divine supply? Who do you listen to? Who speaks into your life? Who corrects you to keep you safe?

When God leads you to them, you need to love them and highly honor that divine supply, not letting anything or anyone separate you from them.

As children, when our parents corrected us, we couldn't just get offended and leave, then go somewhere else to get different parents. No, we stayed with them, and as we submitted to them, we matured and were kept safe.

Even so, if our spiritual parent corrects us, they are helping and protecting us from hardship and failure. No matter what, never allow offense in; don't leave them. We can't just decide to jump from one spiritual parent to another, because only the one God connects us to is anointed to help us.

Just as the devil seeks to separate sheep from their pastor so he can weaken them, the devil will use all kinds of strategies to try to separate someone from their divine supply, because then he can weaken them and their ministry.

Don't let anything or anyone separate you from your divine supply; your future depends on it.

The only time God would redirect us is if the one we are following goes a different direction than God's plan. Paul stated, *"Be ye followers of me, even as I also am* (a follower) *of Christ."* We could read it this way, "Even as, or as long as I follow Christ, you follow me." If they quit following Christ and His plan, then God will redirect us, but we are not authorized to redirect ourselves to someone else.

Clarity of God's Plan

First Kings 17 tells the story of Elijah and the widow woman. God had been supplying for Elijah during a famine; he drank water from a brook, and ravens brought him food. Later, God directed Elijah to go to a certain city where a widow woman would feed him. She was in need of a miracle, so God was giving her a man of God to sow into.

God told Elijah that He had already commanded the widow woman to feed him, but when he arrived, she acted like she didn't know anything about it. She wasn't discerning what God had commanded her. Elijah helped her to recognize and act on what God had commanded her. As she obeyed Elijah's instruction, she received her miracle of supply during the famine.

We need someone who knows God better than us to help us correctly identify and define what God has already said to us. As we stay with our divine supply, we receive understanding and clarity of God's will and plan for our lives.

God said to me in Russia, *"Walking in a 'Double Portion' Anointing* ***demands*** *right fellowship and protecting right connections to the divine supplies in your life."* These divine supplies are not optional, and we should not treat them as such; we are to highly value and honor them.

Chapter 17

A Renewed Mind

While in Russia, God said to me, *"Walking in a 'Double Portion' Anointing calls for great renewing of the mind. An unrenewed area of the mind is the entrance place of defeat."*

A man with a "Double Portion" Anointing is dealing with the mightiest power in existence. Therefore, there is no room for a mind out of agreement with God.

For our minds to agree with God, we must renew them with the Word, which means to take on God's thoughts and His way of thinking.

The faith of God is in our spirits, not our minds. We cannot believe God with our minds; we believe Him with our spirits, our hearts. If our mind is renewed with the Word, it will agree with the faith that's in our spirits, but if our mind is unrenewed, it will hinder the faith that is in our spirits from flowing. Faith in our spirit can flow when our mind agrees, but faith is hindered from flowing when our mind is not in agreement with the Word.

A spiritual giant is one whose heart and mind agrees.

An unrenewed mind will worry, fear, doubt, disbelieve, etc. However, a renewed minds forbids the entrance of those things. The temptation of those things will still come, but the renewed mind forbids their entrance by refusing to entertain those thoughts.

If our minds are troubled in some area, then we know we need to further renew our minds in that area.

The renewing of our minds is something we will have to continue to do for the rest of our lives, for the mind doesn't stay renewed any more than the hair stays combed. Every day we have to put right thinking in place, so that our minds don't revert back to the old way of thinking – that's done by continuing to feed on God's Word and doing it.

A renewed mind agrees with the written Word of God, but it also agrees with what God says to them by His Spirit. A mind that is not renewed will argue and reason against the Word of God, as well as against what God may say to them by His Spirit.

Job 22:21 reads, *"Acquaint now yourself with Him [**agree with God** and show yourself to be conformed to His will] and be at peace; by that [you shall prosper and great] good shall come to you"* (Amplified).

Those who are acquainted with or know God are those who agree with Him. If someone has no interest in living out His will for their life, they don't know Him as they should because they have not brought themselves into agreement with His will.

According to this verse, to agree with God you must "...show yourself to be conformed to His will...," which means to *do* His will. It's not enough to verbally agree with God; our agreement must show up in what we do.

The rest of this verse tells us what great reward and blessing happens to those who agree with God's will and do it – they will be at peace, they will prosper, and great good will come to them. This all belongs to the renewed mind.

A renewed mind knows God and agrees with Him, therefore they are carrying out His perfect will for their lives.

Discerning the Perfect Will of God

It takes a renewed mind to discern what the perfect will of God is for our lives.

Romans 12:2 tells us, *"And be not conformed to this world: but be ye transformed by the renewing of your mind, that ye may prove* (or be able to discern) *what is that good, and acceptable, and perfect, will of God."*

This verse shows us that there are three different levels of God's will.

1. Good – This would describe those who are born again, but never go further with God – but it's good that they are born again.

2. Acceptable or Permissive – This would describe a believer who chooses to follow their own plan in life rather than God's; they are in God's permissive will, meaning He permits them to go their own way. He will bless them as far as He can, but He can only bless them limitedly because they aren't in His perfect will.
3. Perfect – In His perfect will is where believers will walk in and receive God's best for their lives, living the best life. The perfect will of God is *far* above the good and the permissive will of God.

According to Romans 12:2, it's only the renewed mind that can even discern between the good, acceptable, and perfect will of God, so that we can accurately choose the perfect. Those who don't choose God's perfect will for their lives don't have their minds renewed mind as they should.

We must not only be able to discern God's perfect will for our lives, but we must come into agreement with it. When someone is struggling, it's because they're not agreeing with God. When we don't obey God's will for our lives, we will face unnecessary struggles, but when we come into agreement with His will, then we will live the best life.

To be skillful in our call and with our anointing, we must be able to discern God's perfect will for our lives.

When we are walking in the perfect will of God, He will instruct us to do things that the unrenewed mind would falter over, but the renewed mind takes God's thoughts and follows where He leads, obeying Him in all things.

As we progress in walking out God's perfect will for our lives, He will also lead us further into deeper realms of the Spirit. We must have our minds renewed to go further in the Spirit, for an unrenewed mind will draw back from the deeper realms of the Spirit.

It's walking out God's perfect will for our lives that gives us the best life, brings the greatest joy, and bears the most fruit.

Chapter 18

Hearing & Seeing

> While in Russia, God referred to what Jesus said to me the previous night, *"I only say what I HEAR My Father say, I only do what I SEE My Father do.*
>
> *"A 'Double Portion' Anointing calls for keen and accurate hearing and seeing. It calls for great discipline to hold the thoughts, mouth, and actions to what is seen and heard from the Father."*

Jesus did not insert any of His own way of thinking or doing into what God said or showed to Him. He carried things out exactly as God said it to Him or showed it to Him.

If we are to walk as Jesus walked, we must be keen in our hearing and seeing – we must recognize when God is speaking or showing us something. Then we must make sure we are receiving and carrying out those things with accuracy.

Centuries ago, God sent a person with a message to speak to the ruler of France. When they told the ruler what God said he was to do, the ruler asked, "If God has something to say to me, why does He speak to you and not to me?"

Their response was, "Oh, He does. But you don't hear Him because you haven't spent the hours listening for Him that I have."

By spending time in His presence, we will come to recognize when He is speaking.

Try the Spirits

The further we go in the Spirit and pray in the Spirit, the more keen our spirits will become to the Holy Spirit, but we will also become more keen to evil spirits. The devil knows what the Spirit of God sounds like, so he seeks to imitate Him as closely as possible; therefore, it's not always immediately obvious to us who is speaking. That's why we are told to "try the spirits."

It doesn't mean that we are wrong when we may hear a wrong spirit, but we must discern what spirit is speaking to us, the Holy Spirit or an evil spirit.

We are to always go by what we sense in our spirits about what we are hearing. It doesn't matter how dramatic or spectacular an experience may be. It must bear witness with our spirits whether or not it's from God. If it doesn't seem right or set right in your spirit, reject it.

When God speaks to us, everything He speaks will always be in line with His Word. When the devil or evil spirits speak to us, they may use the Word, but it will be a misapplication or misuse of the Word.

We are warned, *"Beloved, believe not every spirit, but try the spirits whether they are of God..."* (1 John 4:1). This means that we are to take the time we need to discern and distinguish who is speaking to us, whether it's the Holy Spirit or an evil spirit. Because it's not always immediately obvious, we are to take the time needed to judge it in light of the Word and with what we sense in our spirits. If it's God, it will bear witness and seem right and good in our spirits.

Don't act on something quickly unless you have taken the time needed to rightly discern who is speaking to you. It's wisdom to wait until you are clear about it. Your wisdom is in waiting.

When an evil spirit is speaking, there may also be a sense of being pushed to act immediately. There may be fearful thoughts trying to push you to act immediately, accusing you that if you don't act immediately you'll miss God or disobey Him.

An evil spirit wants you to disregard any time needed to distinguish who is talking to you because an evil spirit can't pass the test of "trying the spirits." That's why it will try to push you to act immediately, so that you will bypass taking the time needed to "try the spirits."

The Holy Spirit passes the test of "trying the spirits" every time. When you take the time needed to "try the spirits," you are not disobeying or delaying obedience or displeasing God – you're acting on what the Word says to do.

If the Spirit of God is speaking to you, He will not push you to bypass the time needed to distinguish that it's His voice. There is no fear or push when He's leading or dealing with you. If it's the Spirit of God, it will still be the Spirit of God after you've taken the time to discern who is speaking to you.

The spirit of fear will try to pass itself off as the leading of the Spirit, trying to push and press you to act now. If there is something in your spirit that doesn't set right, or something in you that doesn't seem good, reject what you heard.

But when the Spirit of God is speaking to you or showing you something, it will seem good and right in your spirit, even if the devil tries to bombard the mind to get you to do something differently. Just follow the peace and the leading that's in your spirit and disregard the reasonings of the mind.

Stay in the Spirit & Out of the Mental Arena

God said to me, *"A 'Double Portion' Anointing calls for keen and accurate hearing and seeing. It calls for great discipline to hold the thoughts, mouth, and actions to what is seen and heard from the Father."*

Jesus did not insert any of His own way of thinking or His own way of doing into what God said or showed to Him. He carried things out exactly as God said it to Him or showed it to Him.

We are not to add any of our own human thinking and reasoning into what God says and shows to us. We are not to add our own interpretation into what He says or shows us. To be keen and accurate in the Spirit, we are to look to our spirits for any needed clarity of what we hear and see from Him, not try to figure it out or reason it out mentally.

The devil seeks to draw us into the mental arena regarding what God may say or show us so that we will insert either our own thinking or any error he suggests.

On one occasion, God directed me to do something financially. I knew it was God leading me, so I did it. Afterwards, there came a bombardment, accusing me that I had missed it and would suffer financially for it. So I just answered those accusing, fearful thoughts. I told the devil, "No, God told me to do it, and I didn't miss it."

That's what we are to do when the devil tries to trouble us with wrong thoughts. Answer them! And answer them specifically. The devil threatens us with specific thoughts, so we must answer him with specific answers.

Words are a living force, so when the devil speaks, his words will continue to move, circling over us, trying to trouble our minds until we stop them. How do we stop them? We answer them! They won't stop until we answer them.

But God spoke to me about that incident, "Stay in My presence. Stay in the Spirit and out of the mental arena, and the devil won't be able to trouble your mind. In the future, I will be leading you to do things that the devil will try to trouble your mind about. But by staying in My presence, in the Spirit, he won't be able to trouble your mind with those things."

If we hold things God speaks to us or shows us in the mental arena, the devil can trouble us about them or get us to insert a wrong interpretation on them, and then it will miss the mark.

As God said to me, "It calls for great discipline to hold the thoughts, mouth, and actions to what is seen and heard from the Father," so that we don't insert our own thinking into them. We must hold to what God says and shows us without inserting anything of our own into it.

Accuracy in Gifts of the Spirit

When we draw things up into the mental arena, that's when we get into error regarding spiritual things and the operation of spiritual gifts.

For example, if a pastor thinks about or converses about situations a congregation member may be facing, he is handling that in the mental arena. Later, if God wants him to minister to them by a gift of the Spirit (either prophecy, word of wisdom, or word of knowledge), then it's very likely that what he speaks will be tainted by having already handled that in the mental arena. His previous thoughts and conversations can leak into what he ministers to them.

Someone may say, "Well, if it's a gift of the Spirit, then it's always right." Well, the Spirit is always right, but He flows through and manifests through men, who are imperfect vessels. So we can end up inserting something of our own thinking into what the Spirit says to us without realizing it.

Some guest ministers would tell pastors not to tell them anything about what may be going on with them or the church, then if God wanted them to minister by the Spirit, it wouldn't be tainted by a previous conversation on the topic.

It's easy to end up prophesying or ministering out of our own minds if it's regarding something we've been thinking or conversing about a lot. If we are to minister accurately by the Spirit, we have to discipline ourselves to not touch certain things in our thought lives.

Chapter 19

Perfectly Surrendered

God said to me in Russia, *"Walking in the 'Double Portion' Anointing is not a place to be feared, but a place to be sober about – great soberness.*

"To walk in this does not call for a perfect man (without flaws), but for a perfectly-surrendered man."

Anything God calls and anoints us to do is to be done by the power and ability He gives. Zechariah 4:6 tells us, *"...Not by might, nor by power, but by my spirit, saith the Lord of hosts."*

We are not to fear what He calls us to because it's not to be accomplished by our own might, strength, or ability, but by His.

We are to be sober about our part – walking in the Spirit, living full of the Word and the Spirit, and obeying Him in all things. We are also to rest in Him, knowing that He is the One who does the work.

To be perfectly surrendered to Him means that we are fully yielded – having no reservations and holding nothing back – and we are willing and obedient in all things.

Whatever we are called to, whatever He anoints us to do, we have the great honor, joy, and privilege of being a co-laborer with the Lord, and He is the One who empowers and equips us to do our part.

Prayer of Salvation

Heavenly Father, I come to You in the Name of Jesus. Your Word says, *"...him that cometh to me I will in no wise cast out"* (John 6:37). So I know You won't cast me out, but You will take me in, and I thank You for it.

You said in Your Word, *"...If thou shalt confess with thy mouth the Lord Jesus, and shalt believe in thine heart that God hath raised him from the dead, thou shalt be saved. For whosoever shall call upon the name of the Lord shall be saved"* (Rom. 10:9 & 13).

I believe in my heart that Jesus Christ is the Son of God. I believe Jesus died for my sins and was raised from the dead so I can be in right-standing with God. I am calling upon His Name, the Name of Jesus, so I know, Father, that You save me now.

Your Word says, *"...with the heart man believeth unto righteousness; and with the mouth confession is made unto salvation"* (Rom. 10:10). I do believe with my heart, and I confess Jesus now as my Lord. Therefore, I am saved! Thank You, Father.

Please write us and let us know that you have just been born again.
When you write, ask to receive our salvation booklets.

To contact us, please email us at
dm@dufresneministries.org
or write to:
Dufresne Ministries
P.O. Box 1010
Murrieta, CA 92564

How To Be Filled With the Holy Spirit

Acts 2:38 reads, "*...Repent, and be baptized every one of you in the name of Jesus Christ for the remission of sins, and ye shall receive the GIFT of the Holy Ghost.*" The Holy Ghost is a gift that belongs to each one of God's people. Jesus is the gift God gave the whole world, but the Holy Spirit is a gift that belongs only to God's people.

Jesus told His disciples, "*But ye shall receive POWER, after that the Holy Ghost is come upon you: and ye shall be witnesses unto me...*" (Acts 1:8). When you're baptized with the Holy Spirit, you receive supernatural power that enables you to live victoriously.

Indwelling vs. Infilling

When you're born again, you receive the indwelling of the Person of the Holy Spirit. Romans 8:16 tells us, "*The Spirit itself* (Himself) *beareth witness with our spirit, that we are the children of God.*" When you're born again, you know it because the Spirit bears witness with your own spirit that you are a child of God; He confirms it to you. He's able to bear witness with your spirit because He's in you; you are *indwelt* by the Spirit of God.

But the Word of God speaks of another experience subsequent to the new birth that belongs to every believer, and that is to be baptized with the Holy Spirit, or to receive the *infilling* of the Holy Spirit.

God wants you to be full and overflowing with the Spirit. Being filled with the Spirit is likened to being full of water. Just because you had one drink of water doesn't mean you're full of water. At the new birth, you received the indwelling of the Spirit – a drink of water. But now God wants you to be filled to overflowing – be filled with His Spirit, baptized with the Holy Ghost.

> **ACTS 2:1-4**
> **1 And when the day of Pentecost was fully come, they were all with one accord in one place.**
> **2 And suddenly there came a sound from heaven as of a rushing mighty wind, and it filled all the house where they were sitting.**
> **3 And there appeared unto them cloven tongues like as of fire, and it sat upon each of them.**
> **4 And they were all FILLED with the Holy Ghost, and BEGAN TO SPEAK WITH OTHER TONGUES, as the Spirit gave them utterance.**

When these disciples were filled with the Holy Ghost, they began to speak with other tongues as the Spirit gave them utterance; they spoke in a language unknown to them. Today, when a believer is filled with the Holy Ghost, they will speak with other tongues too. These are not words that come from the mind of man, but they are words given by the Holy Spirit; these words float up from their spirit within, and the person then speaks those out.

What is the benefit of being filled with the Holy Ghost with the evidence of speaking in other tongues? First Corinthians 14:2 reads, *"For he that speaketh in an unknown tongue speaketh not unto men, but unto God...."* When you're speaking in other tongues, you're speaking to God – it is a divine means of communicating with your Heavenly Father. This is one of many great benefits.

MATTHEW 7:7-11
7 Ask, and it shall be given you...
8 FOR EVERY ONE THAT ASKETH RECEIVETH...
9 ...what man is there of you, whom if his son ask bread, will he give him a stone?
10 Or if he ask a fish, will he give him a serpent?
11 If ye then, being evil, know how to give good gifts unto your children, HOW MUCH MORE SHALL YOUR FATHER WHICH IS IN HEAVEN GIVE GOOD THINGS TO THEM THAT ASK HIM?

In this passage, Jesus is saying that when you ask God for something, you shall receive it! Believe that He will give you that which you ask for. When you ask God for something good, He won't give you something that will harm you; He will give you the good thing you ask for. The baptism of the Holy Spirit is a good gift, and when you ask God to fill you with the Holy Spirit, you won't receive a wrong spirit; you will receive this good gift, the gift of the Holy Spirit.

Once you receive the gift of the Holy Ghost, you can yield to this gift any time, speaking in other tongues as often as you choose; you don't have to wait for God to move on you. The more you speak in other tongues, the more you will benefit from this gift. By continuing to speak in other tongues on a daily basis, you will be able to maintain a Spirit-filled life; you will live full of the Spirit.

The more you take time to speak in other tongues, the deeper you'll move into the things of God.

(For more teaching on being filled with the Holy Spirit, I recommend the mini-book, *Why Tongues?* by Kenneth E. Hagin.)

Prayer To Receive the Holy Spirit

"Father, I see that the gift of the Holy Spirit belongs to Your children. So, I come to You to receive this gift. I received my salvation by faith, so I receive the gift of the Holy Spirit by faith. I believe I receive the Holy Spirit now! Since I'm filled with the Holy Spirit now, I expect to speak in other tongues as the Spirit gives me utterance, just like those in Acts 2 on the Day of Pentecost. Thank You for filling me with the Holy Ghost."

Now, words that the Spirit of God gives you will float up from your spirit. You are the one who must open your mouth and speak those words out. The words will not come to your mind, but they will float up from your spirit. Speak those out freely.